620.1

Materials Science
CERAMICS

making use of the secrets of matter

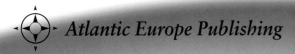

Atlantic Europe Publishing

First published in 2003 by
Atlantic Europe Publishing Company Ltd.

Author
Brian Knapp, BSc, PhD

Art Director
Duncan McCrae, BSc

Senior Designer
Adele Humphries, BA, PGCE

Editors
Mary Sanders, BSc, and Gillian Gatehouse

Illustrations
David Woodroffe

Design and production
EARTHSCAPE EDITIONS

Scanning and retouching
Global Graphics sro, Czech Republic

Print
LEGO SpA, Italy

Materials Science – Volume 4: Ceramics
A CIP record for this book is available from the British Library

ISBN 1 86214 318 8

Acknowledgments
The publishers would like to thank the following for their kind help and advice: *Jack Brettle*; *Jonathan Frankel*; *Peter and Ellie Nalle*; *Steve Rockell and John Crobnick*; *Rolls-Royce plc*; *Pete Thompson*; *Caroline Wise*.

Picture credits
All photographs are from the Earthscape Editions photolibrary except the following: (c=center t=top b=bottom l=left r=right)

British Alcan Aluminium plc 46t; *British Coal* 57; *NASA* COVER background, 42t, 42b; *Rolls-Royce plc* 43t, 43b; *UKAEA Technology* 54.

This product is manufactured from sustainable managed forests. For every tree cut down, at least one more is planted.

Contents

(*Left*) This is the liquid ceramic used for some dental fillings. It is hardened by exposure to ultraviolet light.

1: Introduction

(Above) All minerals—not just silicates (clay)—are ceramics as far as materials science is concerned. These beautiful stones are just as much ceramics as a brick in a wall.

See **Vol. 5: Glass** for more on glass.

(Below) Ceramics tend to be brittle and so can easily be broken with a sharp blow.

The word "CERAMIC" comes from the Greek *keramikos*, meaning potter's clay. In general use the word "ceramic" means anything made of clay that has been hardened by heat. In materials science the word has gradually become to be used more widely and means any material or product, including pottery or brick, that is made from a mineral, and that is crystalline and usually brittle. This definition, which is used in this book, includes minerals such as diamond that have a crystalline structure. It does not include glass, which has a special structure of its own.

In practical terms ceramics are usually hard, strong, brittle solids that will stand up to heavy wear and high temperatures.

Many ceramics do not conduct heat or electricity very well. They do, however, resist reacting with acids, alkalis, and liquids that might dissolve other materials.

Ceramics do not "weather"—that is, unlike metals that tarnish or rust, they do not change when exposed to rain, sunlight, cold, and so on.

Ceramics can also be easily decorated.

Because the definition of ceramics covers a surprisingly large range of materials, from bricks, cups, and saucers to diamond, graphite, and silicon chips, ceramics also have a wide variety of properties. Diamond, for example, conducts heat better than copper, and graphite and zirconium dioxide (zirconia) are excellent conductors of electricity.

Some ceramics, especially when other things are added to them, can also occur in forms that make them less brittle than we might expect.

But whatever the properties of any particular ceramic, its properties are always the result of its chemistry, both in the elements that go into it and the way they are bonded together.

How ceramics are formed

The atoms in a ceramic material are held together in two ways: Neighboring atoms may share electrons (this is called COVALENT BONDING), or they may be held together by electrical attraction (called IONIC BONDING). Both of these types of bond are very strong. In general, it is their strong bonding that gives ceramics their property of hardness, and that also prevents them from changing shape and so makes them brittle.

(Above, left, and below) Natural flint—silicon dioxide—can be broken and cemented into a wall to make a durable and decorative finish. Flint is found as nodules in chalk rock. It can also be fractured to produce a durable and extremely sharp edge, something the Stone Age peoples discovered. The hand ax is among the earliest tools used by mankind.

In some ceramics, such as diamond, all of the bonds are of the types described above. That makes diamond an exceptionally hard material. But in many ceramics layers of crystals are held together by weaker bonds. In the case of graphite sheets of carbon atoms bonded strongly together are held sheet to sheet by much weaker bonds. That is what allows graphite to flake away and be used as a lubricant, even though it is made of carbon atoms just as diamond is (which is used as an abrasive).

(Left and below) The structure of diamond produces an extremely hard material. Its hardness makes it useful for such extreme applications as diamond-tipped saws and drills.

How ceramic crystals are organized

Some ceramics have their atoms packed extremely tightly. This applies to diamonds and compounds such as magnesium oxide, which is made of large metal IONS (which are positive ions, or CATIONS) each surrounded by six smaller oxygen ions (or ANIONS). Since the oxygen ions pack into the spaces between the metal ions very effectively, the compound is very stable. This pattern can only be broken up at very high temperatures, which is why many ceramics can be used in ovens and kilns (and are called REFRACTORY, or high melting, materials).

Some metal ions are surrounded by oxygen ions that are not so tightly bonded. It is also possible to replace some of the oxygens with other ions. This introduction of IMPURITIES to a structure is called DOPING, and it is very important in making some ceramics conduct electricity—it is the basis of the transistor used in silicon chips.

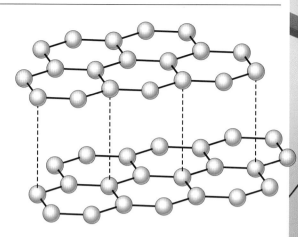

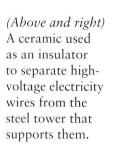

(Above and below) The structure of graphite produces a soft, slippery material. Graphite is used for pencil leads and as a lubricant.

(Above and right) A ceramic used as an insulator to separate high-voltage electricity wires from the steel tower that supports them.

See **Vol. 2: Metals** for more on metals and conductivity.

In some ceramics the metal ions, which are normally centrally placed among all of their surrounding oxygen ions, can be made to move closer to some of the oxygen ions and thus farther from others. This has the effect of making the material able to hold enormous electrical charges. Ceramics of this kind are used as electrical storage devices called CAPACITORS.

Of course, ceramics are normally thought of as INSULATORS, that is, materials that do not conduct electricity, or at best conduct it very poorly. To understand this property, it is best to compare them with metals, which are good conductors of electricity. In a metal the atoms share many of their ELECTRONS, so that electrons can easily move around. The movement of electrons produces an electric current. In ceramics the electrons cannot move around in this way, and so the materials are insulators.

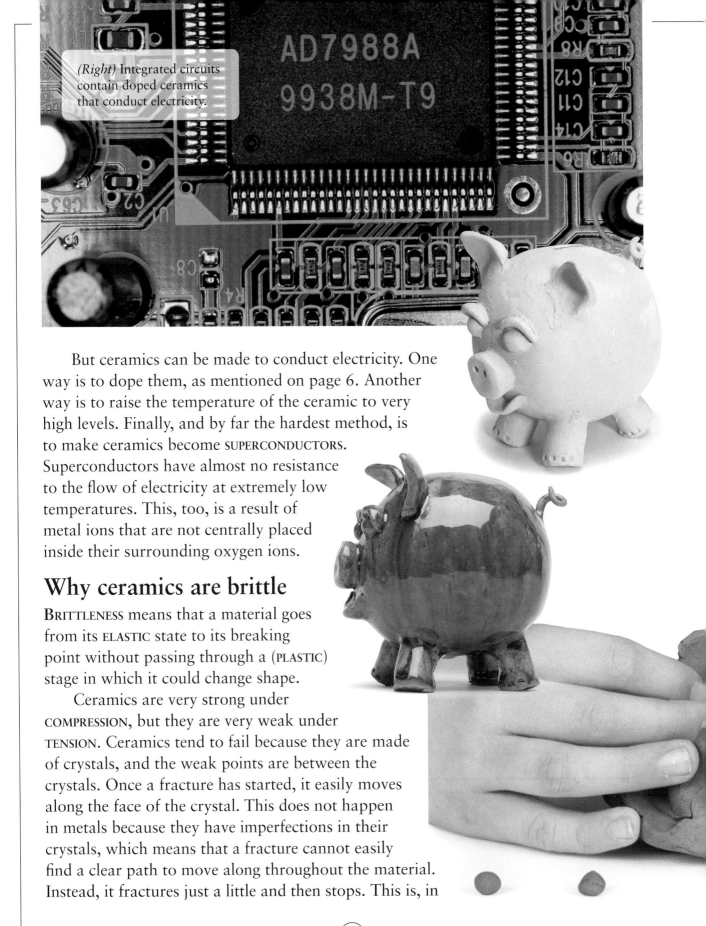

But ceramics can be made to conduct electricity. One way is to dope them, as mentioned on page 6. Another way is to raise the temperature of the ceramic to very high levels. Finally, and by far the hardest method, is to make ceramics become SUPERCONDUCTORS. Superconductors have almost no resistance to the flow of electricity at extremely low temperatures. This, too, is a result of metal ions that are not centrally placed inside their surrounding oxygen ions.

Why ceramics are brittle

BRITTLENESS means that a material goes from its ELASTIC state to its breaking point without passing through a (PLASTIC) stage in which it could change shape.

Ceramics are very strong under COMPRESSION, but they are very weak under TENSION. Ceramics tend to fail because they are made of crystals, and the weak points are between the crystals. Once a fracture has started, it easily moves along the face of the crystal. This does not happen in metals because they have imperfections in their crystals, which means that a fracture cannot easily find a clear path to move along throughout the material. Instead, it fractures just a little and then stops. This is, in

See **Vol. 5: Glass** for more on glass.

(Above, left, and below) The stages in making a durable ceramic. First, the ceramic, in this case clay, is wetted and molded. Then, it is dried and heated. Finally, it is coated with a glaze (a glass solution) and fired in a kiln. It is now hard, resists abrasion, and is watertight. But it is far more brittle than it was when simply soft clay.

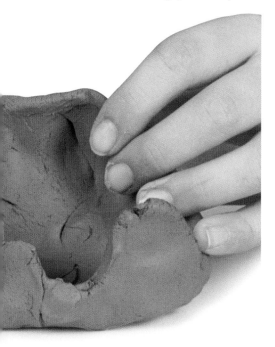

fact, what allows a metal to BEND; bending is internal breaking that only affects a few crystals at a time. As the break begins in a metal and the atoms slip, there are many more places along the fracture where the atoms can bond back again. Breaks are thus both little and temporary, and so the metal can be bent time and time again.

Ceramics have much more perfect crystals than metals; imperfections of the kind common in metals are rare in ceramics. That is why their bonds are stronger and why it is difficult to make a ceramic bend. Also, once the fracture starts, there are no imperfections to keep the fracture from spreading right across the material, and no other places where a slipped atom can bond back again. In fact, slipping brings particles of the same charges side by side, and since like charges repel, helps push the broken parts away.

Glasses, which do not have a crystal structure and so are not regarded as ceramics, are even more likely to fracture under tension than ceramics.

Making ceramics

Glass and metals can both be melted and then be poured into molds. Ceramics cannot be melted and re-formed. If a ceramic is melted, it turns into a glass.

To make a ceramic fit into a mold, it has to be ground into a powder and the powder added to a liquid so that it can be shaped and then heated. This process is called SINTERING, in which the tiny particles bond under heat.

This may seem like a very high-tech affair, but in fact people were doing it in ancient times. When wet clay is molded, it is a powder of tiny clay particles in water. The clay is shaped into cups, bowls, plates, and so on, and then heated in a kiln. Sintering then occurs, the water is driven off, and the clay powder fuses together to make a hard, brittle ceramic. And the result: common cups, bowls, and all of the other materials that we use from day to day.

2: Common ceramics

For thousands of years people have made many things using clay and sand. They are the traditional materials that make up what we normally think of as ceramics—mugs and plates, vases and pots, bricks and roof tiles. The same materials also make up the bulk of cement and concrete.

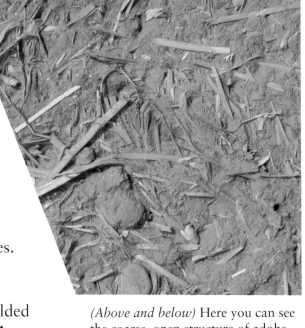

The very first ceramics were probably molded from wet clay and allowed to dry in the sun. ADOBE brick is still made this way. It is not a material of great sophistication, but it can be crafted into some very practical objects, such as adobe houses used throughout the world; skillfully used, it can be turned into beautiful architecture.

(Above and below) Here you can see the coarse, open structure of adobe. The straw acts as fibers, binding the clay and manure together.

Early clay vessels, like adobe houses, had a very big limitation: They were not waterproof and could only be used for a short time before liquid leaked through. Nonetheless, clay bowls and mugs were used as simple drinking vessels for thousands of years. They can be thought of as the original disposable cups.

Needless to say, people looked for ways of making their utensils stronger and harder as well as being watertight. It was probably by accident that people found out that this was just what happened if they threw a fragment of clay onto a fire.

With the knowledge of how heating can transform clay, it became possible to make bricks and roof tiles that would not fall part when it rained.

Clay bricks proved to be good but not very strong. They were improved by adding straw to the brick—thus creating the first REINFORCED FIBER materials.

(Below) Adobe is a kind of mud that is used worldwide for buildings in desert and semidesert areas. It is cheap and easy to make, but it is not waterproof, and so buildings have to be repaired frequently. This is a church made of adobe near Taos, New Mexico.

(Above) The stone blocks in Roman-built Hadrian's Wall, England, are held together with the mortar that the Romans developed. It is still there 2,000 years later.

(Below) Roman pot with coriander seeds. Note dimples of sand grains that were embedded to make an abrasive surface for grinding.

Clay can be shaped and a decoration put on to its surface before it is fired. Thus it provides an easy way for many societies to display and keep examples of their artistic talents. As a result, hardly a pot or plate was made that did not have some form of decoration. This was, incidentally, invaluable for later archaeologists trying to figure out the age of the ceramics (and thus of the societies) whose remains (ARTIFACTS) they found.

Ceramics can be used not just to make things in themselves, but to help make other things of other materials. For example, by making an indentation, or MOLD, in packed sand, molten liquid can be poured in which, on setting, will take the shape of the molded sand. This was one of the first things that people did when the metal age began with the use of bronze some 5,000 years ago.

Then it was discovered that a combination of sand and lime made a material that would set and harden. The Greeks were the first people to discover this new material—which we now call CEMENT—but it was much more widely used by the Romans, who used it in many of their walls.

Although cement, as other ceramics in use at the time, was made of easily available, low-value materials, many of the ceramic products then were costly to buy because of the time that went into creating them by hand. It wasn't until the INDUSTRIAL REVOLUTION (which started in the 18th century) that mechanization dramatically reduced the cost of production.

In the modern world both handmade and mass production ceramics find a market. For most things we use mass-produced ceramics, but some decorative ceramics are handcrafted.

(Above and below) Roman mosaic floor. A mosaic is built up from tiny pieces of tile set in a cement base.

Mosaics were developed by the Romans and have been a popular means of practical decoration ever since. These modern mosaics are in Sydney, Australia (*above*), and Eureka, California (*below*).

Materials for ceramics making

The clay materials for common ceramics are simple and widely available. The materials are also heavy and bulky. As a result, for most of history ceramics have been made near where they were needed. Often, each village had its own potter or brickmaker. Over the years, taking material from the ground to make ceramics has left suitable clay areas pockmarked with shallow pits.

Many people think of clay as a material made of very small particles that, when wet, turns into a sticky mud. However, besides having small particles, clay also contains a range of platelike minerals, and they give clay special properties. These CLAY MINERALS contain aluminum, silicon, and oxygen, and are called aluminosilicates.

A special form of clay mineral, called KAOLINITE, or CHINA CLAY, is not found on the Earth's surface but underground near the sites of extinct volcanoes.

In places that were once magma chambers of volcanoes, hot fluids were able to decompose the granite rocks and turn them into clay.

The great mass of surface clays are found naturally as beds of particles that settled out in ancient lakes or shallow seas. These clays were produced as rainwater decomposed rocks on land, and the clays were then carried by rivers until they reached the still waters of lakes and seas, where they settled out. As these rocks were buried, they were compressed.

Very compressed clays are called shales, but they are not useful in the ceramics industry. What that industry needs are clays that can still be molded.

The important feature of clay particles is that when lubricated by water, they are able to slip over one another yet still hold together. The water does not bind them. Instead, they are bound electrically. This happens because as the clays form, the surface of each clay particle become very slightly negatively charged.

In ordinary water there are many positively charged particles. Calcium in the water is a good source of them. It often comes in the form of tiny positively charged particles (cations). Since opposites attract, the calcium is attracted to the negatively charged surfaces of the clays. The calcium has enough charge to allow it to attach to two clay surfaces at the same time, and that is how the clays come to be held together even though they are waterlogged.

The forces holding them together are, however, not very strong. Thus the combination of particle shape and weak bonds means that the clays can easily be molded, or formed, into new shapes.

The other two main ingredients of common ceramics making are silica (sand) and feldspar. Sand is a filler and provides reinforcing for the clay both when it is wet and once it has been fired and hardened.

Feldspars are similar to clays but also contain sodium, calcium, and potassium ions. When feldspar (as opposed to china clay) is used, it acts as a material called a FLUX, lowering the temperature at which the clay will sinter.

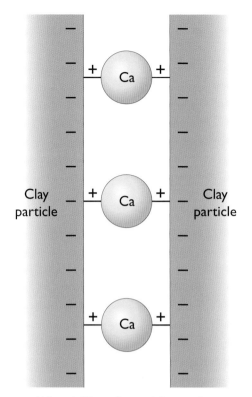

(Above) How clays stick together using calcium ions. Calcium has two positive charges, so one charge can link with the surface of one clay, and the other charge can link with the surface of the other. This locks the particles together.

(Above) Two contrasting colors of bricks (red and gray) create an attractive decorative effect on this building.

Processing the raw materials

Fortunately, much of the raw material for ceramics is readily available and needs fairly little treatment before it can be used. This is in marked contrast to most industries (in the case of metals, for example, the metal has to be extracted from its ore before it can be used) and helps keep down costs.

One of the side effects of using the material straight from the ground is that it provides the opportunities for many attractive regional variations. In bricks and roof tiles, for example, the changing colors between regions reflect the changes in the natural iron staining that occurs on the clays.

Furthermore, natural clays already contain sand and flux, and so they fire easily.

Bricks and tiles are colored. Most tableware is not. Clay dug from the ground may not be suitable for it. Special sources of clay, such as kaolinite (china clay) deposits, must be found. As a result, ceramics intended to have a white color (and sometimes called "whiteware") tend to be made in more restricted locations, and factories are often grouped near a suitable source of material.

In other cases each of the raw materials has to be washed to get rid of staining and impurities.

(Above and below) The color of both bricks and mortar depends on the materials from which they were made. In general, the more iron in them, the stronger the color. This wall is made from a recycled collection of bricks that show the great range of colors that can be obtained.

The brickwork below is from a completely different region than the one above. In this case the bricks are dominated by purple colors.

(Above) Hand making of bricks using just clay and a wooden former is very time consuming.

(Below) Making pottery is an ancient craft using nothing more than wet clay, a potter's wheel, and a great deal of skill.

Once cleaned, clay, sand, and feldspar are blended together with water. The blending determines the final character of the whiteware. Not surprisingly, most of the art of making good wares depends on the skill of the blender.

Clay changes its character depending on how much water is added. The objective is to get a mix that is exactly right for the next stage of manufacture—forming it into a product.

In most cases the ideal water content produces a mixture that can support itself and yet still be easily worked. For factory-made wares the clay is shaped into a long roll and chopped off into suitably sized pieces. Each piece is then fed into a press in which one part of a mold moves against another and squashes the clay into the shape of the mold.

Complicated and irregular shapes can be made using molds, although very simple objects such as bricks and tiles are made by presses.

Pressing has to be done one item at a time. Each product has to be removed from the press before another can be fed in. To increase production of identical items such as bricks, clay is forced through a rectangular-shaped piece of metal called a die. The correctly shaped stream is pushed out of the die as a long strip of clay and simply has to be cut to the right brick length by a blade before being taken off for firing.

It is possible to make clay products from clay that has had so much water added that it has turned into what looks like a liquid (although it is in reality a SUSPENSION). That is what is done in the process called "slip casting."

The suspension is poured into a mold that is made of a POROUS material like plaster. The water is sucked from the clay into the plaster, and the clay then gains solidity and can be taken from the mold and fired.

(Above) The clay suspension is poured into casts made of plaster, and the excess drained off. Once enough moisture has been taken from the body of the clay, the object will have enough rigidity not to deform under its own weight, and the cast can be removed. The clay is then ready for firing.

Firing

The heating of ceramics to make a hard, strong material is called firing. Firing uses lots of heat, and it would be wasteful to also use this heat to dry as well as harden the ceramic. The first stage after molding or casting is therefore for the article to be left to stand in order to dry in the air for a while. This can be speeded up by using low-temperature ovens and fans.

There are two kinds of water associated with clays. One kind is the water between the clays. In dry air it will evaporate. The second kind is water contained inside the clay crystals. This water can only be removed by stronger heating. At the same time, such heating burns off any impurities such as bits of organic matter.

After drying, the clay is fired. The oven, which is called a kiln, is loaded with ware, and it is heated up. Once the batch is sintered, it is taken out, and a new batch put in. However, working batch by batch is not suitable for mass producing articles such as bricks. In the case of large-scale mass production tunnel kilns are used: Continuous belts carry the material slowly to the hottest part of the kiln and then back out again.

Vitrification

The word VITRIFICATION means to turn to glass. It is what happens in the kiln when the edges of the clay platelets begin to turn glassy and fuse together.

During vitrification some of the glass flows into the pores between particles and helps fill them up. Small particles also fuse together with the larger particles. This produces a denser material and also makes the ware watertight. Only then does the clay change permanently

(Below) These crockery items, removed from their casts, have been left to dry for a while before being stacked and put in the batch kiln for firing. The kiln is in the background of the picture. The stacking needs to be done in such a way that the heated air reaches all the items as evenly as possible to reduce the risk of fracturing. An item that is incorrectly fired can disintegrate explosively, damaging many other pieces in the process.

and become hard, strong, and waterproof. The clay also shrinks slightly as the water is driven off.

It is important not to let vitrification go too far, for the secret is just to cause fusing, not melting, or the ware will lose its strength and sag while in the kiln.

The temperatures at which this happens vary between 1,600°C and 3,300°C depending on the materials used in the ceramic.

(Above) The fired items are painted. Hand-painted designs give each item an individual charm. Finally, they are glazed and fired again.

Glazing

Even after firing, the ware is not necessarily watertight (impermeable). To make it completely impermeable, glass is crushed up and suspended in a liquid. This pulverized glass will make a glaze (a protective and decorative coating).

The glass suspension is then painted or sprayed onto the ware, or it can be dipped in a bath of glaze. Glazes can be colored by adding metal oxides.

Glazing needs an additional firing. The firing temperature the second time is high enough to melt the glass (about 1,500°C) but below the temperature that would cause the clays to further vitrify. A glazed product is thus a combination of a ceramic and a glass surface coating. It is sometimes called VITREOUS CHINA.

(Above) The painted items are then dipped in a glaze bath to cover the whole surface. This glaze will be transformed from an OPAQUE coating to a TRANSPARENT protective surface when fired for the last time.

(Left and right) The difference between a glazed and unglazed tile. The unglazed tile (*left*) has a dull surface. The glazed tile to the right has a shiny, glasslike finish (shown clearly above the broken edge).

(Right) As this Mexican design shows, tiles can be beautiful as well as being very practical. They can take frequent wetting and extreme changes in temperature, and they are very strong, making them an ideal building material.

Glazing is an extremely popular finish, and glazed tiles are used decoratively as well as practically in kitchens as work surfaces, as exterior waterproof tiles, as decoration for mosaics, as cups, saucers, toilet bowls, and so on.

(Above) The Chinese have used tiles for many millennia.

(Below) Modern houses frequently use glazed or unglazed tiles for roofing materials.

3: Ceramic products

(Below) Pots, bowls, cups, and plates can all be whitewares. But they may also be EARTHENWARE, STONEWARE, or PORCELAIN depending on how they were made.

In the previous chapter we looked at the basic stages of making any ceramic. We ended by explaining the use of a glass (glazed) surface coat. In this chapter we look in more detail at some of the products of the ceramics industry.

The ceramics industry has a wide range of names for the materials it produces, and some are associated with the type of product manufactured. You will see this as we begin the chapter with the great range of products that can all be grouped under the term "whitewares," not all of which are white!

Whitewares

By "whitewares" we mean ceramics that have a white or off-white color (unless specifically colored) and have been considerably vitrified to make them watertight. They include an enormous range of products from toilet bowls and sinks to cups and saucers, to dentures, and spark-plug ceramics.

All of these products have important properties in common: They are impermeable and so do not let liquids through; they do not react with liquids; they can be formed into complicated shapes; and they are electrical insulators.

To create these properties, it is important both to choose the correct materials and to go through the correct kind of firing.

Although the materials used for whitewares —clay, sand, and feldspar—may seem simple, the exact nature of the three materials and their blending is very important, and there are differences between the types of product they can be made into.

(Above) Ceramic tiles with whiteware toilet bowl and tank. The earthenware has been glazed to make it watertight and also for sanitary purposes. Other similar white earthenware items include sinks. Note that baths are often not ceramic but metal with a glass coating (called vitreous enamel or porcelain enamel).

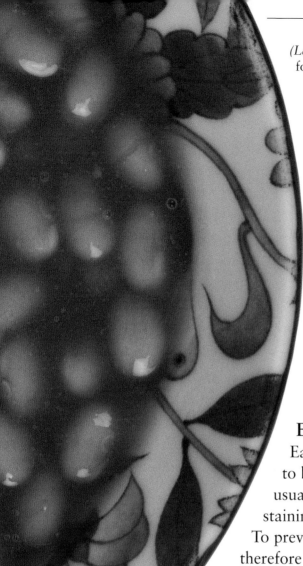

China clay (kaolin) is used almost exclusively because it is the only type of clay from which a white, translucent, glassy ceramic can be made. Kaolin is made of very fine white platelets, with no impurities, especially no iron to stain the clay.

The other benefit of kaolin is that it is a refractory clay, so that it can safely be fired at high temperatures without deforming. As kaolin fires in a kiln, it turns pure white.

Manufacturers of whiteware divide their products into three groups depending on how much the firing has caused the clay to fuse together (vitrify).

Earthenware

Earthenware does not have a glassy finish. If it is to be used to hold liquids, it has to be glazed. It is usually not pure white and is often tinted by iron staining. It is the cheapest form of white tableware. To prevent frequent breaking, it has to be thicker and therefore heavier than other kinds of tableware because it is not fused. Earthenware is also glazed, colored, and used for wall tiles and extensively for sinks and bathroom objects.

(Right) A broken stoneware cup handle. You can see the thick handle typical of stoneware.

Stoneware

Stoneware is partly fuscd clay and has a much finer pore size than earthenware. It is used for tableware, for cooking pots, and for sanitary purposes in the form of drainpipes. Like earthenware, it has to be quite thick to protect it against breakage.

Porcelain

When kaolin is fired to make it glassy and naturally watertight, it is called porcelain. However, there is a difference in quality between true porcelain (which is used to hold chemicals in laboratories and when a very high quality is needed, such as in spark-plugs) and the porcelain used for the objects we generally know as "china."

All porcelains can be made without glazing because their pores are filled with glass in vitrification. They may, however, still be glazed a particular color or finish.

CHINA has great strength and can resist blows much better than other kinds of whiteware. This extra strength is caused by the more thorough internal bonding of the fused clay.

There are many kinds of china, ranging from the best table china, including bone china (which is made with six parts bone ash, four parts china stone, and three and a half parts china clay), through a lower-grade "hotel" china, to some sinks.

(Below) Bone china, a form of porcelain that is strong, hard, and slightly translucent. It can be fashioned into ware that is far more delicate than any other kind of whiteware.

(Above) Porcelain tableware.

Processing whiteware

Each type of whiteware is processed differently. Tiles, plates, cups, and bowls are pressed into shape, while most plumbing fittings, such as basins and toilet bowls, are cast using a clay slurry. Much tableware is also machine formed on a mass-production version of a potter's wheel. This process is called "jiggering."

Because of the huge amount of whiteware made, it is not often batch processed in industrialized countries but rather is sent through tunnel kilns on conveyor belts. Earthenware and stoneware are fired at about 1,200°C and china and other porcelains at 1,300°C.

Kaolin begins to turn glassy over a wide range of temperatures, and so the exact temperature is not critical. For example, the first change to glass begins at about

990°C. The feldspar would all be molten at 1,140°C. But only when the temperature reaches 1,200°C does real glass form. And because the glassy particles are so sticky (viscous), the piece does not tend to warp out of shape. Furthermore, variations in the exact composition of the raw material are also not critical. What these variations do is create slightly different grades of material. That is, the composition and temperature are not as critical here as they are in many other kinds of chemistry. That is what makes the production of whitewares so easy, and why they were some of the first manufactured products.

(Above and below) Bricks are the basis of much housing. Bricks are often used to face a building even if its structure is made of wood.

Ceramics for building

The ceramics used for building are bricks and roofing tiles, paving slabs, and decorative garden stone. They make up about half of all the ceramic wares made worldwide.

(Right) Many houses in historic districts are made of brick. That is because brick is much more durable than wood, and so the brick buildings have often survived while the wooden ones have not.

Bricks were first made about 6,000 years ago. Over time the size and shape of the brick evolved. The main factor influencing the size and shape was ease of handling, though bricks also had to be big enough to create a good "footprint" and so a strong wall.

Because brickmaking is usually a local industry, and exports of bricks are small, the size and shape have not been standardized as they have for many other products. So, wide variation is found across the world.

Making bricks does not require pure components in the same way as in the whiteware industry. Indeed, staining by iron and other metal compounds is welcomed to add an attractive color to the bricks. However, the main concern in making a building ceramic is that it be strong, for houses built with bricks are heavy and put enormous downward stresses on the lower rows (courses) of bricks. Bricks also need to be able to resist weathering by rain, cold, and heat.

The color of bricks depends on the amount of impurities in the mixture and on the way the kiln is operated. Colors ranging from pale yellow through tan, brown, red, and black are possible. However, the metal oxides that cause the color also act as fluxes, helping reduce the temperature at which the clay begins to vitrify.

The purple colors of some bricks are achieved by a process called flashing. It happens at the end of the brickmaking. The bricks are moved into an oven in which there is a gas such as carbon monoxide that reacts with oxygen in the brick and so takes it away from the oxygen in the iron. That changes the iron oxide (from ferric to ferrous oxide), and the brick turns from red to purple.

Bricks are needed in huge quantities for such basic structures as houses. To keep the prices

(Below) Red bricks can be used to form a durable and decorative surface, as shown in this street.

Stages in industrial brickmaking

1. **Winning.** The clay has first to be excavated from the ground. This process is called "winning."

2. **Preparation.** The clay is crushed to break up stones. If the source of clay is shale rock, grinding wheels are used.

3. **Forming.** Water is added to the clay and mixed using rotating blades. This is called "pugging." It makes the clay plastic.

4a. **Stiff-mud process.** Clay is mixed with just enough water to make a moldable material. The clay is then pushed through a die, and rollers add a surface texture. The long rod of textured clay is then cut up using a blade (guillotine). The stiff-mud process produces the strongest bricks.

4b. **Soft-mud process.** Sticky clays, which have a higher water content, are made in batches in molds.

4c. **Dry-press process.** Clays with a water content of less than 10% are used. The clay is pressed into steel molds by a hydraulic ram.

5. **Drying.** When wet clay comes from molding or cutting machines, it must be dried before it can be fired. This happens in ovens whose temperatures are set between 38°C and 204°C. Drying takes between one and two days. The heat for these ovens is waste heat coming from the firing kilns.

6. **Firing and cooling.** Firing takes between two days and a week. Both batch kilns and tunnel kilns take about the same firing time. In the first stage the free water is first evaporated at a temperature of about 204°C. Next, water is taken from the clay water molecules at temperatures of 150°C to 500°C. As the temperature rises to 500–980°C, the clay begins to oxidize, and at 900–1,300°C it vitrifies. Once it has vitrified enough, the bricks are slowly cooled.

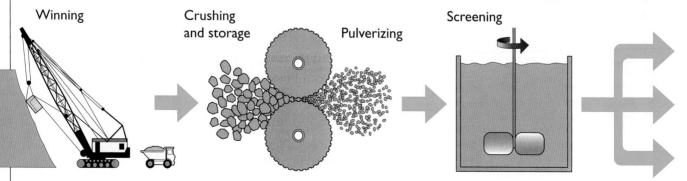

Winning

Crushing and storage

Pulverizing

Screening

(Left) An old brick kiln that is itself made of brick.

of houses as low as possible, it is important to keep the cost down. As a result, natural variability in the texture and color of the mixture is tolerated. It is perhaps just as well that this typical variability happens to provide a welcome visual appeal that people value in their house bricks.

Bricks can be made darker, more waterproof, stronger, and more dense simply by compressing them or firing them at higher temperatures.

Bricks have much more filler and flux than whitewares. Typically, they may contain between a third and a half clay, the rest being made up of quartz (sand) and feldspar flux. This is also a commonly occurring makeup of clayey shales, which means clay dug from the ground can be made directly into bricks.

Clays for brickmaking must have enough plasticity to allow them to be shaped or molded when mixed with water, and they must have sufficient wet and air-dried strength so that they keep their shape after being formed.

Three types of clays are used:

Surface clays are soft. They are readily scooped up by an excavator from the ground after only the overlying soil has been removed.

Shales are clays that have been compressed and formed soft rocks. They are more difficult to use than surface clays.

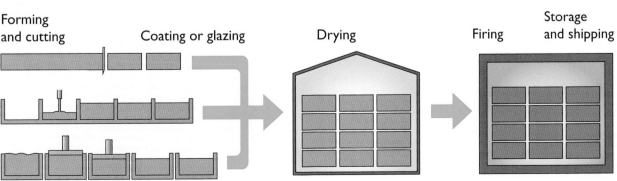

Forming and cutting   Coating or glazing   Drying   Firing   Storage and shipping

Particle sizes of the filler used in bricks made from shale are greater than for whitewares, so the final texture is coarser.

Fire clays are those that can be used in high temperatures. They are clays with fewer impurities than shales or surface clays, and they have more uniform chemical and physical properties.

These clays are unlike metals in that they soften slowly and melt or fuse gradually when heated. That is why firing all ceramics in kilns takes many hours.

Firing bricks

Most bricks are fired in continuous production tunnel kilns, except when they are made on a small scale. Firing temperatures for bricks are typically 1,000°C to 1,100°C lower than for whitewares. Only the edges of the clays turn to glass at these lower temperatures, and the interlocking needles of glass produced hold the sand in place. However, these temperatures, and the length of time of firing are critical. Without proper firing, the bricks would not have the strength they need, and they would crumble under the weight of overlying bricks or break up if wet and then subjected to freezing temperatures. Bricks that are fired for too long are very strong; but too much glass has formed in them, and so they are more brittle and likely to crack under load.

Because so little clay turns to glass in brickmaking, there is little opportunity for the glass to fill in the natural pores in the mixture. Bricks are therefore quite porous (have many small holes) and reasonably permeable (let water seep through). That is why bricks used on the outside of houses are generally protected by the overhangs of roofs (eaves) of buildings. The eaves stick out to keep the walls below mostly dry. Furthermore, a space is usually left between the outer brickwork and the inner building, and a waterproof lining sheet covers the inner framework. In this way water seeping into the brick does not get into the walls of the rooms.

The porosity caused by a mixture of large and small particles does have major advantages. Its

(Above) Terracotta pots, a cheap, robust, and decorative material, especially when set against a contrasting color, such as with the flowerpots in this scene in Mexico.

(Left and below) Terra cotta is a bright red form of pottery that began in the Mediterranean region of Europe.

(Right) Terracotta wall light used for its decorative effect. Like all ceramics, it resists cracking when it is subjected to the heat of the light bulb.

structure makes the brick able to take much larger loads than other common types of ceramic.

Other building ceramics

Besides wall bricks there are several other important categories of building ceramic. TERRA COTTA (a word of Italian origin meaning "baked earth") is a strong, red-brown, porous fired clay. It was the common building material of the ancient Mediterranean world and is now found all over Greece and Rome. It is used to make statues and vases as well as bricks and tiles. Terra cotta has even been used for the decorative shapes (architectural relief) on buildings.

Wall and floor tiles are made of fired clay that has been glazed. They are different from "quarry" tiles, which have been pressed so that the clay is dense and able to withstand wear much better.

Special refractory bricks are used to line chimneys, furnaces, and boilers (see page 32).

Most tiles are glazed. High-fired glazes are produced during the tunnel kiln process. The glaze (crushed glass in a liquid) is sprayed onto the bricks and tiles before they go into the kiln.

Low-fired glazes are used to obtain colors that cannot be produced at high temperatures. In this case there is a two-stage process: The tiles are first fired in the usual way, then the glaze is applied and the tiles refired at a lower temperature.

Glazes are not widely used on bricks because they make the brick impervious and do not allow the surface to breathe. That could leave damp inside a house.

(Above and below) Ceramics will not melt. That allows them to be used when containers are needed that will withstand very high temperatures. This laboratory crucible is made of a ceramic, as is the supporting pipe-clay triangle. Steel and other metal furnaces are also lined with heat-resistant ceramics—special refractory bricks.

Refractory materials

A ceramic is called a refractory (from the French *réfractaire*, meaning "unchanging") when it is able to stand up to very high temperatures before it melts. Refractory materials are widely used to line the interiors of furnaces, kilns, and other devices that process things at high temperatures.

Materials that stand up to high temperatures are also often almost unchanging (inert), meaning that they will not react with other materials when they are hot. This is especially important in a metal or glass furnace, for example, where it is vital to keep out impurities, and where the liquids used are very CORROSIVE.

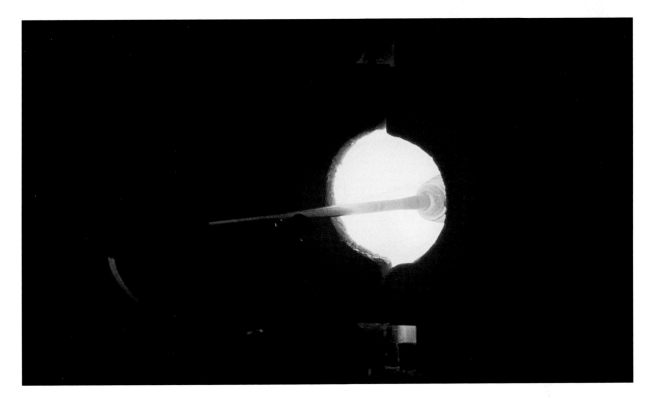

To be a useful refractory, suitable materials must not only have the properties just mentioned, but they must also resist wear (because hot liquids may be churning around against them), and they must resist the tendency to crack when temperatures change rapidly.

Refractories get some of these properties from the way they are fired. Refractories are meant to have quite a coarse texture compared, say, to whitewares and even bricks. Grains are used in refractories that may be millimeters across. Such large grains would be unacceptable in any other kind of ceramic. The large filler grains tend to result in larger pores than in other ceramics. Both of these features make the ceramic less likely to crack when heated or cooled. On the down side, they also make refractories less strong than normal bricks, and so they are not used for building, just for lining furnaces.

One way of preventing the refractory from reacting with the liquid it holds is to make it match the ACIDITY of the liquid. Refractories can be made acid by adding to them sand and fireclay. They can be made alkaline by adding dolomite rock (magnesium carbonate).

(Above) You can see refractory bricks in place around the entrance to this glass-blower's furnace.

Plastering. Plaster uses water to help it set. If it is not made wet enough or the wall not prewetted sufficiently, the plaster will not set properly. (*Below*) Adding a base coat of plaster to insulating bricks. (*Left*) Finishing off the wall with a thin surface coating.

Plaster

Plaster is the material most widely used to provide a durable skin to the inside of buildings. Plaster is gypsum (calcium sulfate $CaSO_4$).

Gypsum is a naturally occurring white mineral. It is found in thick beds where it was once deposited as ancient lake beds evaporated. Gypsum is plentiful and easy and cheap to quarry.

Its main use is as a wall liner. But it is also made into wallboards and used to fill cracks. When it is poured into molds, it is known as plaster of Paris.

Plaster is made by heating gypsum to remove some water. It is then crushed into a fine powder. When water is added, the plaster takes up the water and then sets hard, usually within a couple of hours.

Many grades of plaster are produced by mixing gypsum with a range of SYNTHETIC additives. For example, plasters are made that can be used on very porous surfaces, on surfaces that are not very porous, as a base coat (which contains a lot of crushed quartz), and as a much finer finishing plaster (which contains less quartz that has also been crushed to a finer size).

When surfacing a wall, a plasterer will commonly put on a surface of the coarser plaster about 11 mm thick and then, when it is dry, go over it with a 3-mm coat of finishing plaster.

(*Below*) Gypsum crystal.

Cement

Cement is a word used for many kinds of adhesive, but is most generally applied to the powder used in the building industry.

The main process involved is hydration, which is a chemical reaction of the cement and water. It produces tiny interlocking crystals with a large surface area. Some cements will set and harden under water. They are called hydraulic cements. The most important of them is Portland cement.

Both the ancient Greeks and the Romans knew how to make cement and CONCRETE. The Romans used it widely. The term cement comes from the Latin word *cementum*, meaning "stone chippings," since they were used in the lime-based cement called MORTAR. They had no special name for the binding material itself.

The Romans used volcanic ash mined near the city of Pozzuoli as cement. This ash was rich in clay minerals, the essential ingredient of any cement, since these minerals react with lime in the presence of water to form a hard material.

(Above) Limestone from a nearby quarry is constantly fed to this cement plant by a conveyor belt.

(Below) This very large cement plant has two rotating kilns.

Kiln

Kiln

(Below) A Portland cement plant. The ingredients are crushed and moved through the preheater tower in the foreground. They are then put through the kiln before being ground to a fine cement dust.

(Below) The preheater tower and kiln (the red cylinder).

Quarry
The minerals used in the manufacture of cement must contain four essential elements: calcium, silicon, aluminum, and iron. They have to be in the right proportions.

Limestone plants rely on a nearby quarry of limestone for the calcium. It is frequently mixed with much smaller amounts of clay and sand that provide the other three essential elements. Other materials might also be added to change the properties of the cement.

Crushing
The blasted rock is fed into first crusher where desk-sized rocks are broken down to the size of tennis balls.

Proportioning, blending, and grinding
Raw materials analyzed in the laboratory. They are blended to the right proportions and ground by rollers to a powder ready for the kiln.

Preheater tower
The preheater tower may be more than 70 meters tall. It contains a number of cyclone chambers that mix the ingredients thoroughly. To save energy, the mixture is preheated using leftover hot gases from the kiln.

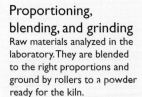

(Left) Quarrying limestone.

Bagging and shipping
A small amount is bagged for minor uses such as mortar, but the majority is transported in bulk by truck, train, or boat.

Clinker cooler and final grinding
The clinker is cooled by forced air as it tumbles over a grate. The cooled clinker is then ground into a superfine gray powder known as Portland cement. The grinding is done by steel balls that are tumbled with the clinker in a rotating mill. The Portland cement is passed through a sieve fine enough to hold water. A small amount of gypsum is added to control the set.

(Right) The kiln (red cylinder).

Clinker

Rotary kiln
The kiln is a huge rotating furnace—a long steel cylinder that is gently sloping and lined with firebrick. This huge kiln makes one to three turns a minute and is the world's largest piece of moving industrial equipment. The kiln is the heart of the cement-making process. As material tumbles along its length, it gets hotter toward the flame, which reaches 1,870°C. The raw materials themselves reach about 1,480°C and become partially molten. At this temperature the calcium and silicon oxides are converted by a number of chemical reactions to calcium silicates, which are the main component of cement. The red-hot particles that leave the kiln are a new substance called "clinker."

Powdered coal and natural gas used for the flame.

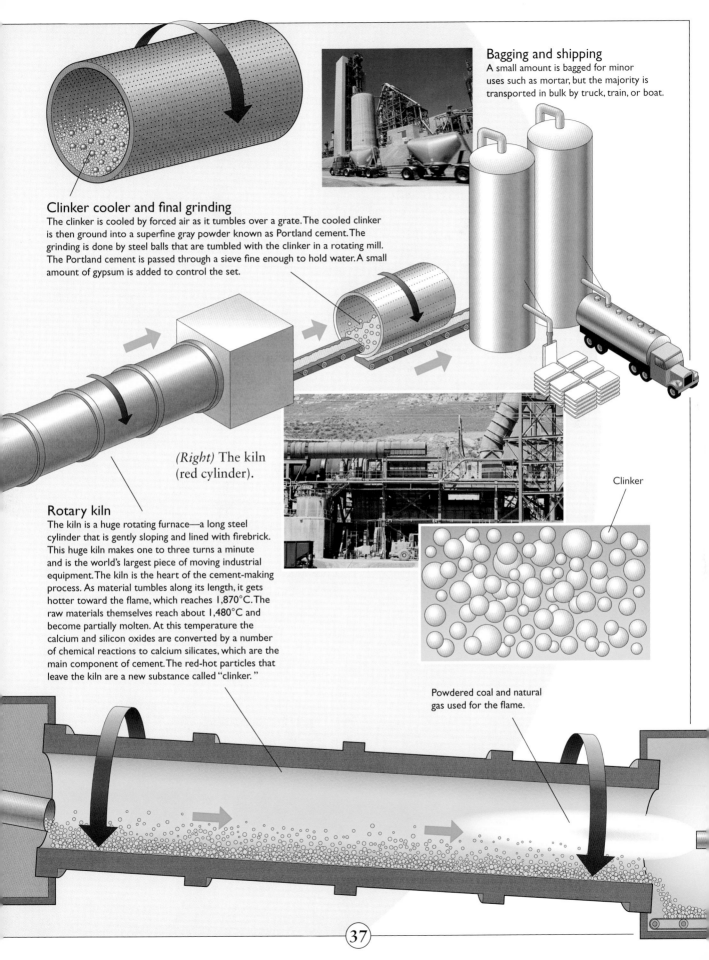

(Above and below) Mortar is a combination of sand and cement.

(Below) Once mixed with water, the mortar forms a stiff paste.

(Below) Within a day the mortar has hardened into a hard rocklike substance.

The first hydraulic (water-setting) cement was developed by John Smeaton, a famous English 18th-century builder of lighthouses. It was made by burning clayey limestone (a natural mixture of lime and clay minerals).

Portland cement was first made in 1824 in the kitchen of a British stone mason, Joseph Aspdin in Leeds. His was the first cement made from different materials mixed together rather than relying on naturally occurring mixtures. He heated a blend of finely ground limestone and clay in his kitchen stove and ground the mixture into a powder. Aspdin named the product Portland cement because it resembled the pale-gray limestone quarried at Portland in Dorset, England.

Portland cement is a mixture of lime (calcium oxide, CaO), silica (silicon dioxide, SiO_2), and alumina (aluminum oxide, Al_2O_3). Small quantities of iron oxide, bauxite (aluminum oxide), and other ingredients may also be added.

The raw materials are limestone, shells or chalk, shale, clay, sand, or iron ore. At the quarries the raw materials are crushed by primary and secondary crushers down to 19 mm across.

At the cement plant the raw materials are mixed together in the correct proportions either dry or as a muddy liquid (slurry). The mixture of raw materials is then fed into the upper end of a tilted rotating cylindrical kiln. The mixture goes through the kiln. Powdered coal or natural gas is forced into the lower end of the kiln and ignited.

Inside the kiln raw materials heat up, and a series of chemical reactions occurs. This is what produces "clinker"—dark-gray pellets that look like marbles. Cooled clinker is combined with gypsum and ground into a fine gray powder. The fine gray powder is Portland cement.

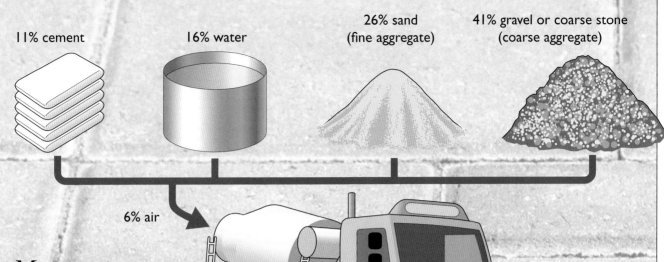

11% cement   16% water   26% sand (fine aggregate)   41% gravel or coarse stone (coarse aggregate)

6% air

Mortar

Cement was never made into a paste on its own because it does not have enough strength, and also because that would waste relatively expensive materials. Instead, a filler is always used. The filler, nearly always building sand, is also a strong material that the cement can trap among its network of crystals.

When sand and cement are mixed and then made into a paste using water, the result is a material suited to bonding bricks. It is called "mortar."

Mortars used by the Romans are still intact today.

(Above) Ready-mixed cement contains the typical cement mixture combined with some additives that delay the start of curing and allow time for the truck to reach its destination.

Concrete

Concrete is a mixture of Portland cement, water, and stones of various sizes (known as aggregates). The Portland cement paste coats the surface of the aggregates. Once the cement has been mixed with water, a chemical reaction called hydration occurs, and the cement hardens and gains strength to form the rocklike mass known as concrete.

After concrete has been poured, it must be kept moist and free from frost or excessive heat. This is called "CURING." Curing allows the process called hydration to work properly on the cement. The tiny cement crystals grow as they take up water and

(Above) Concrete can be made into bricks and used for paving. It is cheaper than conventional brick. This concrete has been colored for added decorative effect.

trap the aggregate. In this way the correct structure develops inside the concrete. During the curing process concrete is often covered with plastic to protect it from frost and heat. Most of the hydration and strength gain take place within the first month of concrete's life cycle, but hydration continues at a slower rate for many years. Concrete continues to get stronger as it gets older.

A concrete mixture that does not have enough paste to fill all the gaps between the stones is difficult to work with and produces rough, honeycombed surfaces and porous concrete. A mixture with an excess of cement paste is easy to work with and

(Above and below) Reinforced concrete is very common in large-scale construction. The bridge below and the skyscraper pillars above are being built using concrete reinforced with steel bars inside the concrete. The steel bars help provide flexibility to an otherwise brittle material.

(Left) Concrete forms the core of this skyscraper. If you look at a city, what you mostly see is concrete and road surface materials.

(*Above*) Resurfacing a road. Tar used as an adhesive to hold stone chippings onto the road surface.

(*Above*) Concrete road surfaces may be hard, but they are brittle and produce a relatively high level of tire noise.

produces a smooth surface, but it may shrink a lot. A proper mix is about 10 to 15% cement, 60 to 75% aggregate, and 15 to 20% water. Trapped air in many concrete mixes may also take up another 5 to 8%.

Road materials

The wearing surfaces of road are all ceramics in material science terms. Usually they are in the form of chips of stone bonded together with a tarlike substance. The tar-bound surface is known as tarmacadam (or tarmac for short) and is the dark street covering that is so common.

Alternative road surfaces are less common either because they are more expensive and less durable (as is the case with paving slabs), or they have less attractive properties (as is the case with concrete roads). Concrete roads in particular have the disadvantage of amplifying the noise of tires. As a result, they are unpopular with people who live close to busy roads.

4: Advanced ceramics

Ceramics have been used since earliest times to make buildings, pots, plates, and so on, as we have seen in the first parts of this book. However, in recent years research has shown that there is much more that can be made from ceramic materials. Advanced ceramics all require a detailed scientific knowledge of how to make a ceramic, which is why they are called "advanced."

We depend on advanced ceramics in all kinds of places, from the loudspeakers in our hi-fi to the blades of a jet engine, to the heat-resisting tiles on the space shuttle.

In advanced ceramics, although many of the manufacturing processes are the same as for common ceramics, naturally occurring raw materials are rarely used. Instead, all of the raw materials have themselves been made, and they are of very special composition.

Preparing the ceramics

Many advanced ceramics are made into objects that are small and need the highest level of precision in manufacturing as well as evenness of composition. A silicon chip is an example of such an advanced ceramic.

This change of scale requires quite different methods of making a ceramic, or at least a different level of accuracy. For example, advanced ceramics work with extremely fine-

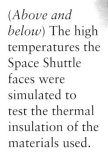

(*Above and below*) The high temperatures the Space Shuttle faces were simulated to test the thermal insulation of the materials used.

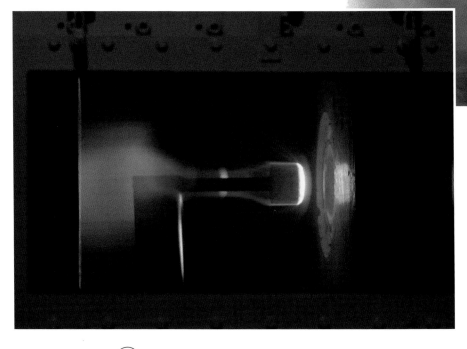

grained powders. Most ceramic powders have grains smaller than a micron (a millionth of a meter). That is smaller than the size of many ordinary clays.

Even mixing is also extremely difficult to achieve by simple techniques such as stirring. As a result, special chemical methods are used. For example, the materials are dissolved in a solution and then PRECIPITATED again. This produces very fine particles that are very evenly mixed. Alternatively, a solution containing the ceramic can be freeze-dried (in a way not unlike freeze-drying coffee) by spraying it into a freezing environment. The sprayed liquid immediately forms very tiny frozen crystals. The spray can also be directed into an oven. The liquid evaporates, and the dissolved materials settle out as a fine powder.

Making the powders into useful things

Once the powders have been made, they have to be turned into useful products. That can be achieved by pressing them into a mold or by turning them into a muddy liquid and casting them, just as is done to clay. In general, however, the molding and casting are very precise. Often the powders are mixed with a RESIN (a plastic substance), which sets as soon as the mixture has been extruded through a die. In this way, for example, tiny honeycomb frames are produced in which the platinum of a catalytic converter can be sprayed. The walls of this ceramic frame are less than a tenth of a millimeter thick.

See **Vol. I: Plastics** for more on plastics.

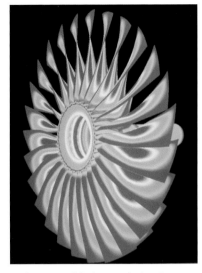

(Above and below) Blades for a turbine can be made from advanced ceramics.

Another way is to cast a slurry of the ceramic onto a tape made of a nonstick material such as Teflon. This slurry then sets, and the tape and the ceramic are rolled up into a reel for later use.

Sintering

In ordinary ceramics heating causes some of the ends of the clays to turn glassy, and that helps hold the ceramic together. It also begins to fill in any pores and so makes the ceramic denser. This is called "sintering," and it is the process that strengthens and hardens the ceramic.

Sintering does not happen in advanced ceramics because they are not made of clays, and because the particles are so much smaller.

When advanced ceramics are heated, the particles literally change shape, with some material moving to places where particles are touching. The touching parts then get fused together.

Ceramics and electronics and optics

We know about ceramics as insulators. They are used, for example, to keep electric wires away from the utility poles that support them. But in the last half century people have discovered a wide range of other ways for ceramics to be used in our everyday lives—although we might not notice it. For example, a simple toaster may now contain a small piece of ceramic that controls when it switches off. A ceramic may store charge inside your computer (it is called a ceramic capacitor); it may be used in your electronic scales (where the change in shape of a ceramic sends out an electrical signal); or ceramic may be found in loudspeakers and in microphones (where it is used as a powerful magnet). Ceramics are also made into lasers and optical switches. In fact, the list of ceramic applications is proving to be both exciting and almost endless.

(Far right and above) Ceramics used for generating electricity from sunshine.

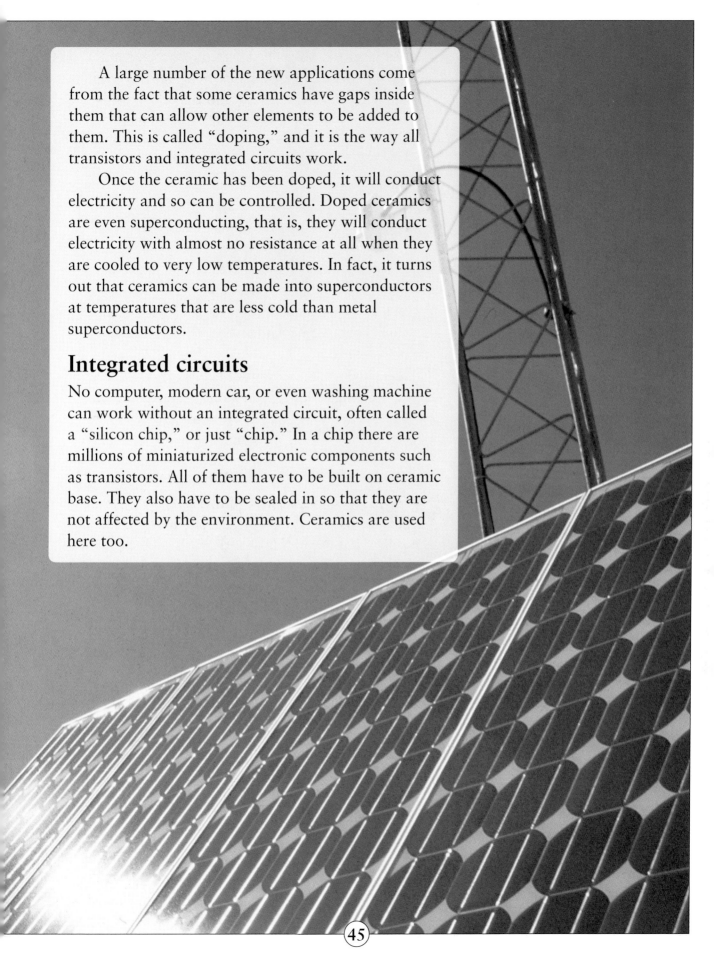

A large number of the new applications come from the fact that some ceramics have gaps inside them that can allow other elements to be added to them. This is called "doping," and it is the way all transistors and integrated circuits work.

Once the ceramic has been doped, it will conduct electricity and so can be controlled. Doped ceramics are even superconducting, that is, they will conduct electricity with almost no resistance at all when they are cooled to very low temperatures. In fact, it turns out that ceramics can be made into superconductors at temperatures that are less cold than metal superconductors.

Integrated circuits

No computer, modern car, or even washing machine can work without an integrated circuit, often called a "silicon chip," or just "chip." In a chip there are millions of miniaturized electronic components such as transistors. All of them have to be built on ceramic base. They also have to be sealed in so that they are not affected by the environment. Ceramics are used here too.

Alumina

The main ceramic material used in electronics is called alumina (aluminum oxide, Al_2O_3). It is a strong material with good insulating properties; it does not corrode, and it seals well to other materials. But it has its drawbacks. It is not good at drawing away heat. This is a problem because chips warm up in use. If they are sealed in by alumina, there is no way for the heat to get out except through the alumina. If the heat cannot get out, the electronics overheat and break down.

To make a base for a chip, a thin film of alumina is created by draping a paste containing alumina powder onto a tape and then heating the tape. The mixture is 99.5% alumina, the rest being magnesia (MgO) and silica (SiO_2). The additives turn glassy when they are heated. They stick the alumina powder together and the components of the chip to the base. The tape is usually a film of about 1 to 2 mm depending on what is needed.

(Above) Alumina powder.

Ceramic capacitors

Capacitors are tiny devices designed to store electricity in an electronic circuit. A capacitor consists of two metal plates separated by a material that does not conduct electricity. Ceramics do not conduct electricity and make ideal capacitors. Nine out of ten of all modern capacitors are ceramics.

Most ceramic capacitor-separating materials are made of barium titanate ($BaTiO_3$). It is made by mixing and then firing powders of barium carbonate and titanium dioxide. They are first spread onto a tape and then punched out of the tape. After that they are fired.

To make the capacitor, two wafer-thin palladium or palladium-silver alloy electrodes are cemented to opposite surfaces of the ceramic. These metals have a melting point that is higher than the firing temperature of the ceramic (1,250°C). This means that the capacitor can be fired with its electrodes in place. Leads are then

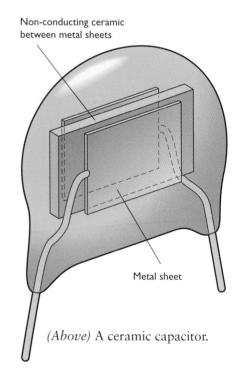

Non-conducting ceramic between metal sheets

Metal sheet

(Above) A ceramic capacitor.

(Right) Ceramic capacitors (the brown disks without the colored bands).

See **Vol. I: Plastics** for more on plastic.

soldered to the electrodes. The whole ceramic and electrode combination is then sealed inside a plastic.

Recently it has been possible to develop new ceramics that fire at lower temperatures. As a result, copper or nickel electrodes can be used in place of the expensive palladium ones.

Ceramic capacitors also form the heart of computer memory chips—RAMs and DRAMs.

Piezoelectrics

PIEZOELECTRICS are materials that produce an electric voltage when they are pushed, pulled, or twisted. The same ceramic used in a capacitor will also produce a voltage when a force is applied to it. This happens because stress on the material makes electrons in it move around. The movement of electrons produces an electric current.

(Left) Piezoelectric igniters are common in gas stoves.

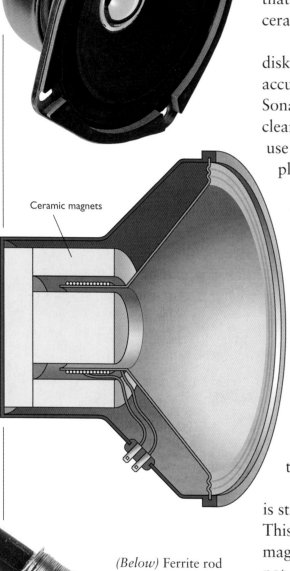

(Left) Magnetic ceramics are used in some loudspeakers.

Ceramic magnets

(Below) Ferrite rod aerial from a radio.

Quartz is the most important natural material that has piezoelectric properties. Many synthetic ceramics have also been made with these properties.

Such materials are extremely widely used. Thin disks of a crystal can be made to vibrate extremely accurately. They form the heart of a quartz watch. Sonar (detecting objects under water) and ultrasonic cleaning (as in a dentist's plaque-cleaning drill) also use piezoelectric crystals. Even pick-ups on record players and microphones use such disks.

In the home doorbells and gas stove igniters work using piezoelectric effects of ceramics.

Magnetic ceramics

Some metal oxides behave just like iron magnets. They are called FERRITES. A common use for ferrites has been as cores in aerials (ferrite rods) for portable radios and in tuning coils mounted on circuit boards. Most coils are tuned by moving their ferrite rods. Other uses for ferrites include permanent magnets, loudspeakers, transformers, and recording and playback heads on camcorders, VCRs, and tape recorders.

If you think that a magnet made out of rock is strange, then look at a piece of natural lodestone. This naturally magnetic rock (geologists call it magnetite) is a naturally occurring iron oxide. It is not a piece of iron.

Metals other than iron can also be turned into magnetic ceramic materials.

Ferrites are made using iron oxide, nickel-iron oxide, and manganese-iron oxide. The powders are pressed into shape and then fired so that sintering takes place in just the same way as in other ceramics.

Ferrites that retain their magnetism after being magnetized are called "hard ferrites." Hard ferrites are used as permanent magnets. Their uses include magnetic inserts in refrigerator door seals, in microphones and loudspeakers, in motors, especially cordless varieties, and also in cars.

Ferrites that do not retain their magnetism are called "soft ferrites." They are commonly used in electrical transformers. One place where they are found in this role is around the necks of cathode ray tubes (television screens), where they help form the picture on the screen.

Magnetic ceramics are also widely used to provide permanent storage of information in computers. All magnetic tapes, whether for video, audio, or computer data, are plastic coated with ferrites. They can be seen in the brown coating on the tape. Hard disks and floppy disks similarly have coatings of ferrite. The ferrites can be magnetized by passing over magnetic read and write heads. More often than not, these heads are also made from ferrite.

Paint containing ferrites can coat military aircraft and make them "invisible" to radar. This is part of the recently developed "stealth" technology.

(Below) Iron oxide powder is stuck to a plastic tape and used as a cassette for audio and video recording and playback.

Ceramics and optics

Most crystals are transparent. However, when they are in the form of powders, they are not transparent because the powders scatter light. But as single crystals many are more transparent than glass.

Crystals of ceramics have been used as superior forms of camera lenses. Many high-quality camera lenses are not made of glass but of the mineral fluorite. This produces clearer pictures, especially at high magnifications when used with zoom lenses.

Sapphire (crystalline aluminum oxide) is a very hard ceramic. A single industrially grown crystal can be cut into thin sheets and used where glass would get scratched and cause problems. One such application is the bar code window at supermarket checkouts. A single sheet of sapphire covers the reader window.

The very bright lights that are used in sports stadiums or in street lights are not enclosed in glass. Under high-temperature conditions glass would fail. Instead, a transparent ceramic of alumina (aluminum oxide) and magnesium oxide is used. It also goes into the "glass" bulb in a sodium discharge tube, the common amber-colored light in most street lights and the mercury vapor lights in sports stadiums. These lights are not only bright, they are also several times more efficient in their use of energy than any other kind of bulb. That is why they are found so widely despite their color.

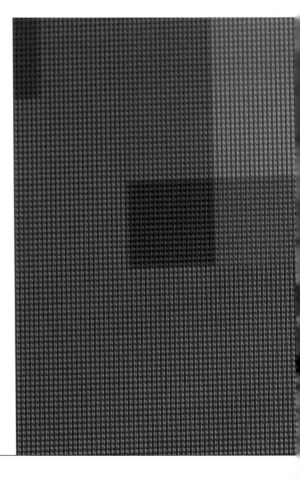

(Above) This digital video camera uses a fluorite lens for sharpness of image.

Ceramics as pigments

Ceramics have long been used as PIGMENTS in paints and glazes. That is, fine powdered ceramics have been used as the coloring agent.

Their value is that some ceramics (particularly those derived from the RARE EARTHS and TRANSITION METALS) absorb all kinds of light except over a very narrow band. They reflect on this band, producing color.

Cobalt aluminate and cobalt silicate are blue; tin-vanadium oxide and zirconium-vanadium oxide are yellow, for instance.

Because they are almost inert (unreactive) and only change at very high temperatures, these powdered ceramics can be used at high temperatures, such as when firing a pot in a kiln.

(Above) Paints contain ceramics as pigments.

See **Vol. 6: Dyes, paints, and adhesives** *for more on dyes and pigments.*

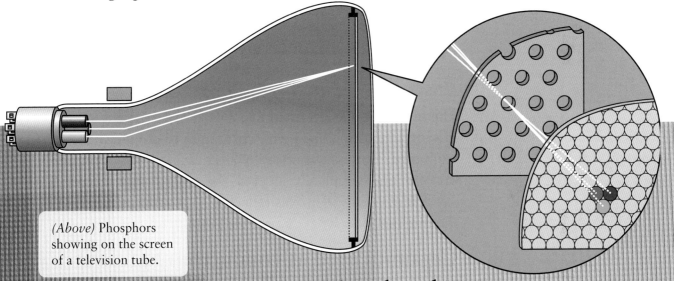

(Above) Phosphors showing on the screen of a television tube.

Ceramics phosphors

However, ceramics can also be used to give out light, not just reflect it. Materials that give out light are called PHOSPHORS. Phosphors are found in fluorescent lights and as the colored dots on a television screen.

Phosphors are ceramics that emit light when they are activated by heat, electricity, X-rays, or light. The light they send out is in a very narrow band, and so they produce very precisely colored light. Phosphors of this kind are ceramics that contain added metals. They are referred to as doped ceramics.

Lead-activated calcium tungstate is a blue phosphor, manganese-activated zircon is a green phosphor, lead- or manganese-activated calcium silicate is yellow, and europium-activated yttrium vanadate is red.

In a cathode ray tube a powder of phosphors is deposited on the inside of the glass screen. When a beam of electrons reaches the phosphors, they glow in their distinctive colors (red, blue, and green). Different energy beams make each of the different phosphors glow. In this way one beam makes red phosphors glow, while another makes blue phosphors glow.

Fluorescent tubes are coated on the inside with calcium halophosphate. The tubes contain a mixture of mercury vapor and an inert gas. When electricity is sent through the tube, the mercury vapor gives out ultraviolet light. We don't see these wavelengths, but they energize the phosphor coating, which then glows white.

Lasers

The first laser was invented in 1960. It used a single crystal of synthetic ruby doped with chromium to amplify light from a flash bulb. The crystal was contained between two mirrors, one completely silvered, the other partly silvered.

In action the light was reflected back and forth between the mirrors, developing a narrow beam.

Ceramics used as conductors

Most ceramics are very good insulators. That is why they are used in such roles as insulators between electric wires and the pylons that support them. Electricity substations also used porcelain ceramics for the same purpose. However, there are some ceramics that conduct electricity.

In ceramics the electrons that would flow, for example, in a metal and thereby conduct electricity are firmly held in place. But if special impurities are included in the ceramic, they can act as donors or acceptors of electrons. That allows ceramics to be used as resistors in electronic circuits and as heating elements in stoves and boilers.

Some ceramics, such as lead oxide (PbO) and ruthenium dioxide (RuO_2), are among the best conductors. These materials are used as resistive films in microelectronic circuits.

The best conductors are based on mixtures of indium oxide (In_2O_3) and tin oxide (SnO_2). They are also transparent. They are used for the liquid crystal displays (LCDs) now common on flat-screen computer monitors and TVs.

The conducting properties described above are all recent developments. But conducting ceramics have been used as heating elements for a long time. They are found in cooking burners, for example. They are known as GLASS CERAMIC.

Sensors

Ceramics are used in a wide range of sensors. Thermistors are one example. A thermistor is a resistor that varies in resistance with temperature.

Thermistors can be used as safety cutout devices to stop overheating. Some toasters have them. Thermistors also appear as fuel-level sensors in gas tanks. Electricity flowing through a thermistor makes it warm up. If the thermistor is in a full tank, the heat escapes from the thermistor faster than if it is partly exposed (if the tank is not completely full). The change in temperature of the thermistor causes a change in resistance, and it can be changed into a reading on a dashboard dial.

Carbon monoxide gas sensors also use ceramics. In this case the ceramic is tin oxide. In the presence of carbon monoxide tin oxide changes its conducting properties. That can trigger an alarm.

This kind of sensor can also detect other harmful gases. It is widely present in chemical laboratories.

Zirconia doped with calcium makes an oxygen sensor to detect the amount of oxygen flowing into a car engine. For the engine to work at peak performance, a specific amount of fuel has to mix with the oxygen. The sensor can detect the level, and the amount of air allowed into the engine can be varied constantly. It also prevents too high a level of air going right through the engine and harming the catalytic converter on the exhaust pipe.

See **Vol. 5: Glass** for more on glass ceramic.

(Above and below) Liquid crystal displays are conducting ceramics.

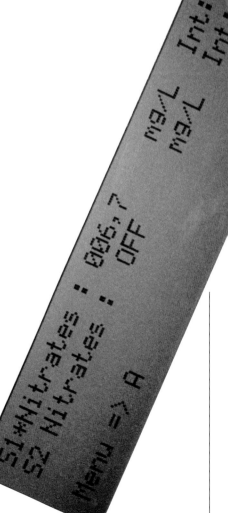

Nuclear ceramics

The nuclear power industry has adopted a wide range of ceramics both as part of the fuel and as containers for radioactive waste.

Fuel pellets are made from uranium or plutonium oxide. When the fuel is spent, the radioactive fuel can be immobilized by encasing it in glass, cement, or other stable ceramic material.

Uranium and plutonium oxides are very suitable as fuel rods, not only because they are radioactive, but also because they melt at very high temperatures and so are stable in the reactor. They are also very resistant to radiation damage.

Pellets are made by crushing uranium ore and then pressing it into shape before sintering it at very high temperature (1,700°C).

Making ceramics for nuclear applications is much harder than it is for most other industries because the reactors work at very high temperatures, many of the liquids are corrosive, and the material is constantly being bombarded with radioactivity.

Bioceramics

Ceramics have many advantages for medical purposes; when they are used in this way, they are referred to as BIOCERAMICS.

Surgeons and those fitting artificial limbs and dentures often need materials that are hard, that are strong especially when pulled or crushed, and that will not crack (suffer from fatigue) or easily chip. Materials also have to stand up to long-term wear; they must not shrink or swell much with temperature or when in liquids. Materials must not let liquids, gases, or life molecules in or out, and they must not corrode when constantly surrounded by the body's fluids. At the same time, the materials must not cause allergic reactions or be toxic to the body. These are tougher demands than for any other kind of use.

Bioceramics can replace bones. Alumina is often used for hip and knee replacements as well as to stand

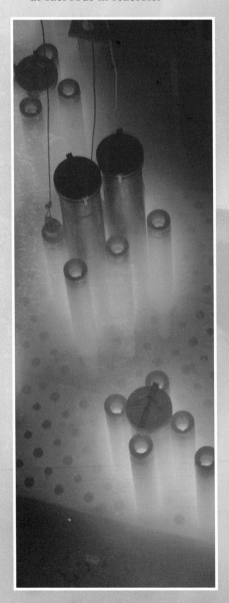

(Below) Ceramics containing radioactive materials are used as fuel rods in reactors.

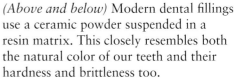

in for bone pieces (for example, when rebuilding face bone) because it does not corrode, it does not wear out, and it has great strength.

However, it is also possible to use POROUS CERAMICS as a kind of scaffolding holding up parts while natural bone growth takes place through the ceramic. Some of these materials become completely reabsorbed into the body when their job is done. They are therefore thought of as temporary ceramics. Some ceramics bond with bones. They are called "bioactive ceramics." They are used in such non-load-bearing places as implants in the middle ear.

In dentistry ceramics play a major role, mostly in combination with resins. Resins are now being used much more widely as fillings in teeth. They can be colored to match the existing teeth much more easily than earlier types of fillings.

The BINDER is a resin, and the filler is pulverized quartz or another hard material. They are used primarily as fillings on the surfaces of teeth rather than at places where grinding action occurs.

Another place that ceramics are used is as cements for holding AMALGAMS in place.

(Above and below) Modern dental fillings use a ceramic powder suspended in a resin matrix. This closely resembles both the natural color of our teeth and their hardness and brittleness too.

The filling paste is applied to the cavity in a tooth through the nozzle of an applicator (*above*). Excess is removed, and the filling is smoothed. It is then hardened quickly using white light, as demonstrated below. Seconds later, and the filling is hard and ready to be drilled to make an exact fit for the tooth.

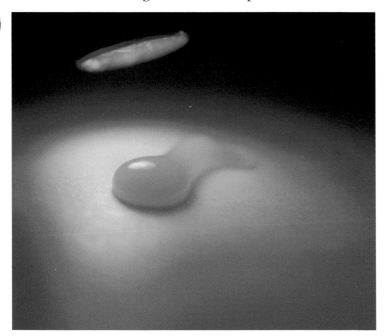

See **Vol. 1: Plastics** *for more on resins.*

Dental cements have to be strong and not cause problems with the gums. They also have to be able to bond well with tooth bone. Zinc phosphate is one common cement. Dental cements have the added advantage that as insulators, they can protect nerves from the highly conductive metal amalgams used in grinding positions. Both can serve as insulating bases to protect tissues from heat or cold. Zinc oxide is also used in a solution of a plastic resin.

Crowns and other artificial dentures are made of porcelain fused to metal. The underlying frame is metal, with the surface layers porcelain, all held in place by cement. Here is an example of metal being used for its strength and to withstand breaks, while the porcelain is used for its appearance.

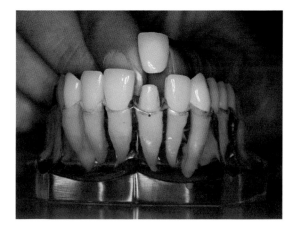

(*Above*) These porcelain ceramic tooth caps make beautiful copies of teeth. However, high-tech materials like this are expensive.

Ceramics that resist wear

Many ceramics are used in extremely demanding places where wear and tear are heavy. If the wrong materials are chosen, rubbing and scuffing can quickly wear out the ceramic part and force an expensive replacement.

Ceramics are used because they are hard and chemically unreactive. But to be really useful, they must also be able to stand up to heat either by swelling and shrinking very little or by being able to transfer away the heat.

The most widely used wear-resistant material is alumina. It has the properties needed and the advantage that it is cheap to make. However, it is possible to improve

(Below) Better saw and grinder blades are coated with diamond, aluminum oxide, tungsten carbide, or silicon carbide. This dramatically increases their life and lets them cut into materials that are harder than the steel of the blade (for example, other ceramics).

on alumina by using composites. One of them is silicon carbide and a base of silica. The grains in this material are not as liable to come loose as in alumina. That is important because when any grain gets loose, it becomes a piece of "grit" and is an abrasive likely to cause damage in a short time.

Ceramics can be toughened by using fibers of other materials such as glass and carbon.

Ceramics are often used to hold liquids, especially if they are corrosive. In these cases ceramics go into valves and pipes, pump parts, and seals.

Ceramics are also important in making high-temperature DIES, such as, for example, to draw wires. Here the dies need to be both tough and heat resistant.

GRAPHITE is an example of a ceramic used as a lubricant. The layered structure of graphite means that it readily flakes. The flakes themselves are very strong, but the bonds between flakes are weak. As a result, the flakes can prevent wear, and they do not wear themselves. Graphites are especially valuable where oils would cause mess (for example, door locks) or at high temperatures, when oils would break down.

Hard-wearing ceramics are also found in the home. Ceramic taps contain valves where one finely ground ceramic disk moves past another in order to control the flow of water. These valves wear in and work better with time rather than wearing out. Ceramic balls are also found in the end of roller ball pens.

Wear-resistant ceramics are also found in many parts of a car. For example, they are the major component of a catalytic converter, which reduces pollution from exhausts. The converter's active ingredient is platinum metal. But it is very expensive. To keep down the cost, the platinum is sprayed as a fine layer on a scaffold of ceramic. The ceramic is either made into pellets or given a honeycomb structure. Pellets are made from alumina and honeycombs from cordierite (a magnesium clay mineral).

Set Glossary

ACID RAIN: Rain that falls after having been contaminated by acid gases produced by power plants, vehicle exhausts, and other man-made sources.

ACIDITY: The tendency of a liquid to behave like an acid, reacting with metals and alkalis.

ADDITION POLYMERIZATION: The building blocks of many plastics (or polymers) are simple molecules called monomers. Monomers can be converted into polymers by making the monomers link to one another to form long chains in head-to-tail fashion. This is called addition polymerization or chain polymerization. It is most often used to link vinyl monomers to produce, for example, PVC, or polyvinyl chloride polymer.
See also **CONDENSATION POLYMERIZATION**

ADHESIVE: Any substance that can hold materials together simply by using some kind of surface attachment. In some cases this is a chemical reaction; in other cases it is a physical attraction between molecules of the adhesive and molecules of the substance it sticks to.

ADOBE: Simple unbaked brick made with mud, straw, and dung. It is dried in the open air. In this form it is very vulnerable to the effects of rainfall and so is most often found in desert areas or alternatively is protected by some waterproof covering, for example, thatch, straw, or reeds.

ALKALI: A base, or substance that can neutralize acids. In glassmaking an alkali is usually potassium carbonate and used as a flux to lower the melting point of the silica.

ALKYD: Any kind of synthetic resin used for protective coatings such as paint.

ALLOY: A metal mixture made up of two or more elements. Most of the elements used to make an alloy are metals. For example, brass is an alloy of copper and zinc, but carbon is an exception and used to make steel from iron.

AMALGAM: An alloy of mercury and one or more other metals. Dentist's filling amalgam traditionally contains mercury, silver, and tin.

AMPHIBIOUS: Adapted to function on both water and land.

AMORPHOUS: Shapeless and having no crystalline form. Glass is an amorphous solid.

ANION: An ion with a negative charge.

ANNEALING: A way of making a metal, alloy, or glass less brittle and more easy to work (more ductile) by heating it to a certain temperature (depending on the metal), holding it at that temperature for a certain time, and then cooling to room temperature.

ANODIZING: A method of plating metal by electrically depositing an oxide film onto the surface of a metal. The main purpose is to reduce corrosion.

ANTICYCLONE: A region of the Earth's atmosphere where the pressure is greater than average.

AQUEOUS SOLUTION: A substance dissolved in water.

ARTIFACT: An object of a previous time that was created by humans.

ARTIFICIAL DYE: A dye made from a chemical reaction that does not occur in nature. Dyes made from petroleum products are artificial dyes.

ARTIFICIAL FIBER: A fiber made from a material that has been manufactured, and that does not occur naturally. Rayon is an example of an artificial fiber.
Compare to **SYNTHETIC**

ATMOSPHERE: The envelope of gases that surrounds the Earth.

ATOM: The smallest particle of an element; a nucleus and its surrounding electrons.

AZO: A chemical compound that contains two nitrogen atoms joined by a double bond and each linked to a carbon atom. Azon compounds make up more than half of all dyes.

BARK: The exterior protective sheath of the stem and root of a woody plant such as a tree or a shrub. Everything beyond the cambium layer.

BAROMETER: An instrument for measuring atmospheric pressure.

BASE METAL: Having a low value and poorer properties than some other metals. Used, for example, when describing coins that contain metals other than gold or silver.

BAST FIBERS: A strong woody fiber that comes from the phloem of plants and is used for rope and similar products. Flax is an example of a bast fiber.

BATCH: A mixture of raw materials or products that are processes in a tank or kiln. This process produces small amounts of material or products and can be contrasted to continuous processes. Batch processing is used to make metals, alloys, glass, plastics, bricks, and other ceramics, dyes, and adhesives.

BAUXITE: A hydrated impure oxide of aluminum. It is the main ore used to obtain aluminum metal. The reddish-brown color of bauxite is caused by impurities of iron oxides.

BINDER: A substance used to make sure the pigment in a paint sticks to the surface it is applied to.

BIOCERAMICS: Ceramic materials that are used for medical and dental purposes, mainly as implants and replacements.

BLAST FURNACE: A tall furnace charged with a mixture of iron ore, coke, and limestone and used for the refining (smelting) of iron ore. The name comes from the strong blast of air used during smelting.

BLOWING: Forming a glass object by blowing into a gob of molten glass to form a bubble on the end of a blowpipe.

BOLL: The part of the cotton seed that contains the cotton fiber.

BOILING POINT: The temperature at which a liquid changes to a vapor. Boiling points change with atmospheric pressure.

BOND: A transfer or a sharing of electrons by two or more atoms. There are a number of kinds of chemical bonds, some very strong, such as covalent bonding and ionic bonding, and others quite weak, as in hydrogen bonding. Chemical bonds form because the linked molecules are more stable than the unlinked atoms from which they are formed.

BOYLE'S LAW: At constant temperature and for a given mass of gas the volume of the gas is inversely proportional to the pressure that builds up.

BRITTLE: Something that has almost no plasticity and so shatters rather than bends when a force is applied.

BULL'S EYE: A piece of glass with concentric rings marking the place where the blowpipe was attached to the glass. It is the central part of a pane of crown glass.

BUOYANCY: The tendency of an object to float if it is less dense than the liquid it is placed in.

BURN: A combustion reaction in which a flame is produced. A flame occurs where gases combust and release heat and light. At least two gases are therefore required if there is to be a flame.

CALORIFIC: Relating to the production of heat.

CAMBIUM: A thin growing layer that separates the xylem and phloem in most plants, and that produces new cell layers.

CAPACITOR: An electronic device designed for the temporary storage of electricity.

CAPILLARY ACTION, CAPILLARITY: The process by which surface tension forces can draw a liquid up a fine-bore tube.

CARBOHYDRATES: One of the main constituents of green plants, containing compounds of carbon, hydrogen, and oxygen. The main kinds of carbohydrate are sugars, starches, and celluloses.

CARBON COMPOUNDS: Any compound that includes the element carbon. Carbon compounds are also called organic compounds because they form an essential part of all living organisms.

CARBON CYCLE: The continuous movement of carbon between living things, the soil, the atmosphere, oceans, and rocks, especially those containing coal and petroleum.

CAST: To pour a liquid metal, glass, or other material into a mold and allow it to cool so that it solidifies and takes on the shape of the mold.

CATALYST: A substance that speeds up a chemical reaction but itself remains unchanged. For example, platinum is used in a catalytic converter of gases in the exhausts leaving motor vehicles.

CATALYTIC EFFECT: The way a substance helps speed up a reaction even though that substance does not form part of the reaction.

CATHODIC PROTECTION: The technique of protecting a metal object by connecting it to a more easily oxidizable material. The metal object being protected is made into the cathode of a cell. For example, iron can be protected by coupling it with magnesium.

CATION: An ion with a positive charge, often a metal.

CELL: A vessel containing two electrodes and a liquid substance that conducts electricity (an electrolyte).

CELLULOSE: A form of carbohydrate. *See* **CARBOHYDRATE**

CEMENT: A mixture of alumina, silica, lime, iron oxide, and magnesium oxide that is burned together in a kiln and then made into a powder. It is used as the main ingredient of mortar and as the adhesive in concrete.

CERAMIC: A crystalline nonmetal. In a more everyday sense it is a material based on clay that has been heated so that it has chemically hardened.

CHARRING: To burn partly so that some of a material turns to carbon and turns black.

CHINA: A shortened version of the original "Chinese porcelain," it also refers to various porcelain objects such as plates and vases meant for domestic use.

CHINA CLAY: The mineral kaolinite, which is a very white clay used as the basis of porcelain manufacture.

CLAY MINERALS: The minerals, such as kaolinite, illite, and montmorillonite, that occur naturally in soils and some rocks, and that are all minute platelike crystals.

COKE: A form of coal that has been roasted in the absence of air to remove much of the liquid and gas content.

COLORANTS: Any substance that adds a color to a material. The pigments in paints

and the chemicals that make dyes are colorants.

COLORFAST: A dye that will not "run" in water or change color when it is exposed to sunlight.

COMPOSITE MATERIALS: Materials such as plywood that are normally regarded as a single material, but that themselves are made up of a number of different materials bonded together.

COMPOUND: A chemical consisting of two or more elements chemically bonded together, for example, calcium carbonate.

COMPRESSED AIR: Air that has been squashed to reduce its volume.

COMPRESSION: To be squashed.

COMPRESSION MOLDING: The shaping of an object, such as a headlight lens, which is achieved by squashing it into a mold.

CONCRETE: A mixture of cement and a coarse material such as sand and small stones.

CONDENSATION: The process of changing a gas to a liquid.

CONDENSATION POLYMERIZATION: The production of a polymer formed by a chain of reactions in which a water molecule is eliminated as every link of the polymer is formed. Polyester is an example.

CONDUCTION: (i) The exchange of heat (heat conduction) by contact with another object, or (ii) allowing the flow of electrons (electrical conduction).

CONDUCTIVITY: The property of allowing the flow of heat or electricity.

CONDUCTOR: (i) Heat—a material that allows heat to flow in and out of it easily. (ii) Electricity—a material that allows electrons to flow through it easily.

CONTACT ADHESIVE: An adhesive that, when placed on the surface to be joined, sticks as soon as the surfaces are placed firmly together.

CONVECTION: The circulating movement of molecules in a liquid or gas as a result of heating it from below.

CORRODE/CORROSION: A reaction usually between a metal and an acid or alkali in which the metal decomposes. The word is used in the sense of the metal being eaten away and dangerously thinned.

CORROSIVE: Causing corrosion, that is, the oxidation of a metal. For example, sodium hydroxide is corrosive.

COVALENT BONDING: The most common type of strong chemical bond, which occurs when two atoms share electrons. For example, oxygen O_2.

CRANKSHAFT: A rodlike piece of a machine designed to change linear into rotational motion or vice versa.

CRIMP: To cause to become wavy.

CRUCIBLE: A ceramic-lined container for holding molten metal, glass, and so on.

CRUDE OIL: A chemical mixture of petroleum liquids. Crude oil forms the raw material for an oil refinery.

CRYSTAL: A substance that has grown freely so that it can develop external faces.

CRYSTALLINE: A solid in which the atoms, ions, or molecules are organized into an orderly pattern without distinct crystal faces.

CURING: The process of allowing a chemical change to occur simply by waiting a while. Curing is often a process of reaction with water or with air.

CYLINDER GLASS: An old method of making window glass by blowing a large bubble of glass, then swinging it until it forms a cylinder. The ends of the cylinder are then cut off with shears and the sides of the cylinder allowed to open out until they form a flat sheet.

DECIDUOUS: A plant that sheds its leaves seasonally.

DECOMPOSE: To rot. Decomposing plant matter releases nutrients back to the soil and in this way provides nourishment for a new generation of living things.

DENSITY: The mass per unit volume (for example, g/c^3).

DESICCATE: To dry up thoroughly.

DETERGENT: A cleaning agent that is able to turn oils and dirts into an emulsion and then hold them in suspension so they can be washed away.

DIE: A tool for giving metal a required shape either by striking the object with the die or by forcing the object over or through the die.

DIFFUSION: The slow mixing of one substance with another until the two substances are evenly mixed. Mixing occurs because of differences in concentration within the mixture. Diffusion works rapidly with gases, very slowly with liquids.

DILUTE: To add more of a solvent to a solution.

DISSOCIATE: To break up. When a compound dissociates, its molecules break up into separate ions.

DISSOLVED: To break down a substance in a solution without causing a reaction.

DISTILLATION: The process of separating mixtures by condensing the vapors through cooling. The simplest form of distillation uses a Liebig condenser arranged with just a slight slope down to the collecting vessel. When the liquid mixture is heated and vapors are produced, they enter the water cooled condenser and then flow down the tube, where they can be collected.

DISTILLED WATER: Water that has its dissolved solids removed by the process of distillation.

DOPING: Adding an impurity to the surface of a substance in order to change its properties.

DORMANT: A period of inactivity such as during winter, when plants stop growing.

DRAWING: The process in which a piece of metal is pulled over a former or through dies.

DRY-CLEANED: A method of cleaning fabrics with nonwater-based organic solvents such as carbon tetrachloride.

DUCTILE: Capable of being drawn out or hammered thin.

DYE: A colored substance that will stick to another substance so that both appear to be colored.

EARLY WOOD: The wood growth put on the spring of each year.

EARTHENWARE: Pottery that has not been fired to the point where some of the clay crystals begin to melt and fuse together and is thus slightly porous and coarser than stoneware or porcelain.

ELASTIC: The ability of an object to regain its original shape after it has been deformed.

ELASTIC CHANGE: To change shape elastically.

ELASTICITY: The property of a substance that causes it to return to its original shape after it has been deformed in some way.

ELASTIC LIMIT: The largest force that a material can stand before it changes shape permanently.

ELECTRODE: A conductor that forms one terminal of a cell.

ELECTROLYSIS: An electrical-chemical process that uses an electric current to cause the breakup of a compound and the movement of metal ions in a solution. It is commonly used in industry for purifying (refining) metals or for plating metal objects with a fine, even metal coat.

ELECTROLYTE: An ionic solution that conducts electricity.

ELECTROMAGNET: A temporary magnet that is produced when a current of electricity passes through a coil of wire.

ELECTRON: A tiny, negatively charged particle that is part of an atom. The flow of electrons through a solid material such as a wire produces an electric current.

ELEMENT: A substance that cannot be decomposed into simpler substances by chemical means, for example, silver and copper.

EMULSION: Tiny droplets of one substance dispersed in another.

EMULSION PAINT: A paint made of an emulsion that is water soluble (also called latex paint).

ENAMEL: A substance made of finely powdered glass colored with a metallic oxide and suspended in oil so that it can be applied with a brush. The enamel is then heated, the oil burns away, and the glass fuses. Also used colloquially to refer to certain kinds of resin-based paint that have extremely durable properties.

ENGINEERED WOOD PRODUCTS: Wood products such as plywood sheeting made from a combination of wood sheets, chips or sawdust, and resin.

EVAPORATION: The change of state of a liquid to a gas. Evaporation happens below the boiling point.

EXOTHERMIC REACTION: A chemical reaction that gives out heat.

EXTRUSION: To push a substance through an opening so as to change its shape.

FABRIC: A material made by weaving threads into a network, often just referred to as cloth.

FELTED: Wool that has been hammered in the presence of heat and moisture to change its texture and mat the fibers.

FERRITE: A magnetic substance made of ferric oxide combined with manganese, nickel, or zinc oxide.

FIBER: A long thread.

FILAMENT: (i) The coiled wire used inside a light bulb. It consists of a high-resistance metal such as tungsten that also has a high melting point. (ii) A continuous thread produced during the manufacture of fibers.

FILLER: A material introduced in order to give bulk to a substance. Fillers are used in making paper and also in the manufacture of paints and some adhesives.

FILTRATE: The liquid that has passed through a filter.

FLOOD: When rivers spill over their banks and cover the surrounding land with water.

FLUID: Able to flow either as a liquid or a gas.

FLUORESCENT: A substance that gives out visible light when struck by invisible waves, such as ultraviolet rays.

FLUX: A substance that lowers the melting temperature of another substance. Fluxes are use in glassmaking and in melting alloys. A flux is used, for example, with a solder.

FORMER: An object used to control the shape or size of a product being made, for example, glass.

FOAM: A material that is sufficiently gelatinous to be able to contain bubbles of gas. The gas bulks up the substances, making it behave as though it were semirigid.

FORGE: To hammer a piece of heated metal until it changes to the desired shape.

FRACTION: A group of similar components of a mixture. In the petroleum industry the light fractions of crude oil are those with the smallest molecules, while the medium and heavy fractions have larger molecules.

FRACTIONAL DISTILLATION: The separation of the components of a liquid mixture by heating them to their boiling points.

FREEZING POINT: The temperature at which a substance undergoes a phase change from a liquid to a solid. It is the same temperature as the melting point.

FRIT: Partly fused materials of which glass is made.

FROTH SEPARATION: A process in which air bubbles are blown through a suspension, causing a froth of bubbles to collect on the surface. The materials that are attracted to the bubbles can then be removed with the froth.

FURNACE: An enclosed fire designed to produce a very high degree of heat for melting glass or metal or for reheating objects so they can be further processed.

FUSING: The process of melting particles of a material so they form a continuous sheet or solid object. Enamel is bonded to the surface of glass this way. Powder-formed metal is also fused into a solid piece. Powder paints are fused to the surface by heating.

GALVANIZING: The application of a surface coating of zinc to iron or steel.

GAS: A form of matter in which the molecules take no definite shape and are free to move around to uniformly fill any vessel they are put in. A gas can easily be compressed into a much smaller volume.

GIANT MOLECULES: Molecules that have been formed by polymerization.

GLASS: A homogeneous, often transparent material with a random noncrystalline molecular structure. It is achieved by cooling a molten substance very rapidly so that it cannot crystallize.

GLASS CERAMIC: A ceramic that is not entirely crystalline.

GLASSY STATE: A solid in which the molecules are arranged randomly rather than being formed into crystals.

GLOBAL WARMING: The progressive increase in the average temperature of the Earth's atmosphere, most probably in large part due to burning fossil fuels.

GLUE: An adhesive made from boiled animal bones.

GOB: A piece of near-molten glass used by glass-blowers and in machines to make hollow glass vessels.

GRAIN: (i) The distinctive pattern of fibers in wood. (ii) Small particles of a solid, including a single crystal.

GRAPHITE: A form of the element carbon with a sheetlike structure.

GRAVITY: The attractive force produced because of the mass of an object.

GREENHOUSE EFFECT: An increase in the global air temperature as a result of heat released from burning fossil fuels being absorbed by carbon dioxide in the atmosphere.

GREENHOUSE GAS: Any of various gases that contribute to the greenhouse effect, such as carbon dioxide.

GROUNDWATER: Water that flows naturally through rocks as part of the water cycle.

GUM: Any natural adhesive of plant origin that consists of colloidal polysaccharide substances that are gelatinous when moist but harden on drying.

HARDWOOD: The wood from a nonconiferous tree.

HEARTWOOD: The old, hard, nonliving central wood of trees.

HEAT: The energy that is transferred when a substance is at a different temperature than that of its surroundings.

HEAT CAPACITY: The ratio of the heat supplied to a substance compared with the rise in temperature that is produced.

HOLOGRAM: A three-dimensional image reproduced from a split laser beam.

HYDRATION: The process of absorption of water by a substance. In some cases hydration makes a substance change color, but in all cases there is a change in volume.

HYDROCARBON: A compound in which only hydrogen and carbon atoms are present. Most fuels are hydrocarbons, for example, methane.

HYDROFLUORIC ACID: An extremely corrosive acid that attacks silicate minerals such as glass. It is used to etch decoration onto glass and also to produce some forms of polished surface.

HYDROGEN BOND: A type of attractive force that holds one molecule to another. It is one of the weaker forms of intermolecular attractive force.

HYDROLYSIS: A reversible process of decomposition of a substance in water.

HYDROPHILIC: Attracted to water.

HYDROPHOBIC: Repelled by water.

IMMISCIBLE: Will not mix with another substance, for example, oil and water.

IMPURITIES: Any substances that are found in small quantities, and that are not meant to be in the solution or mixture.

INCANDESCENT: Glowing with heat, for example, a tungsten filament in a light bulb.

INDUSTRIAL REVOLUTION: The time, which began in the 18th century and continued through into the 19th century, when materials began to be made with the use of power machines and mass production.

INERT: A material that does not react chemically.

INORGANIC: A substance that does not contain the element carbon (and usually hydrogen), for example, sodium chloride.

INSOLUBLE: A substance that will not dissolve, for example, gold in water.

INSULATOR: A material that does not conduct electricity.

ION: An atom or group of atoms that has gained or lost one or more electrons and so developed an electrical charge.

IONIC BONDING: The form of bonding that occurs between two ions when the ions have opposite charges, for example, sodium ions bond with chloride ions to make sodium chloride. Ionic bonds are strong except in the presence of a solvent.

IONIZE: To change into ions.

ISOTOPE: An atom that has the same number of protons in its nucleus, but that has a different mass, for example, carbon 12 and carbon 14.

KAOLINITE: A form of clay mineral found concentrated as china clay. It is the result of the decomposition of the mineral feldspar.

KILN: An oven used to heat materials. Kilns at quite low temperatures are used to dry wood and at higher temperatures to bake bricks and to fuse enamel onto the surfaces of other substances. They are a form of furnace.

KINETIC ENERGY: The energy due to movement. When a ball is thrown, it has kinetic energy.

KNOT: The changed pattern in rings in wood due to the former presence of a branch.

LAMINATE: An engineered wood product consisting of several wood layers bonded by a resin. Also applies to strips of paper stuck together with resins to make such things as "formica" worktops.

LATE WOOD: Wood produced during the summer part of the growing season.

LATENT HEAT: The amount of heat that is absorbed or released during the process of changing state between gas, liquid, or solid. For example, heat is absorbed when liquid changes to gas. Heat is given out again as the gas condenses back to a liquid.

LATEX: A general term for a colloidal suspension of rubber-type material in water. Originally for the milky white liquid emulsion found in the Para rubber tree, but also now any manufactured water emulsion containing synthetic rubber or plastic.

LATEX PAINT: A water emulsion of a synthetic rubber or plastic used as paint. *See* **EMULSION PAINT**

LATHE: A tool consisting of a rotating spindle and cutters that is designed to produce shaped objects that are symmetrical about the axis of rotation.

LATTICE: A regular geometric arrangement of objects in space.

LEHR: The oven used for annealing glassware. It is usually a very long tunnel through which glass passes on a conveyor belt.

LIGHTFAST: A colorant that does not fade when exposed to sunlight.

LIGNIN: A form of hard cellulose that forms the walls of cells.

LIQUID: A form of matter that has a fixed volume but no fixed shape.

LUMBER: Timber that has been dressed for use in building or carpentry and consists of planed planks.

MALLEABLE: Capable of being hammered or rolled into a new shape without fracturing due to brittleness.

MANOMETER: A device for measuring liquid or gas pressure.

MASS: The amount of matter in an object. In common use the word weight is used instead (incorrectly) to mean mass.

MATERIAL: Anything made of matter.

MATTED: Another word for felted. *See* **FELTED**

MATTER: Anything that has mass and takes up space.

MELT: The liquid glass produced when a batch of raw materials melts. Also used to describe molten metal.

MELTING POINT: The temperature at which a substance changes state from a solid phase to a liquid phase. It is the same as the freezing point.

METAL: A class of elements that is a good conductor of electricity and heat, has a metallic luster, is malleable and ductile, and is formed as cations held together by a sea of electrons. A metal may also be an alloy of these elements and carbon.

METAL FATIGUE: The gradual weakening of a metal by constant bending until a crack develops.

MINERAL: A solid substance made of just one element or compound, for example, calcite minerals contain only calcium carbonate.

MISCIBLE: Capable of being mixed.

MIXTURE: A material that can be separated into two or more substances using physical means, for example, air.

MOLD: A containing shape made of wood, metal, or sand into which molten glass or metal is poured. In metalworking it produces a casting. In glassmaking the glass is often blown rather than poured when making, for example, light bulbs.

MOLECULE: A group of two or more atoms held together by chemical bonds.

MONOMER: A small molecule and building block for larger chain molecules or polymers (mono means "one" and mer means "part").

MORDANT: A chemical that is attracted to a dye and also to the surface that is to be dyed.

MOSAIC: A decorated surface made from a large number of small colored pieces of glass, natural stone, or ceramic that are cemented together.

NATIVE METAL: A pure form of a metal not combined as a compound. Native metals are more common in nonreactive elements such as gold than reactive ones such as calcium.

NATURAL DYES: Dyes made from plants without any chemical alteration, for example, indigo.

NATURAL FIBERS: Fibers obtained from plants or animals, for example, flax and wool.

NEUTRON: A particle inside the nucleus of an atom that is neutral and has no charge.

NOBLE GASES: The members of group 8 of the periodic table of the elements: helium, neon, argon, krypton, xenon, radon. These gases are almost entirely unreactive.

NONMETAL: A brittle substance that does not conduct electricity, for example, sulfur or nitrogen.

OIL-BASED PAINTS: Paints that are not based on water as a vehicle. Traditional artists' oil paint uses linseed oil as a vehicle.

OPAQUE: A substance through which light cannot pass.

ORE: A rock containing enough of a useful substance to make mining it worthwhile, for example, bauxite, the ore of aluminum.

ORGANIC: A substance that contains carbon and usually hydrogen. The carbonates are usually excluded.

OXIDE: A compound that includes oxygen and one other element, for example, Cu^2O, copper oxide.

OXIDIZE, OXIDIZING AGENT: A reaction that occurs when a substance combines with oxygen or a reaction in which an atom, ion, or molecule loses electrons to another substance (and in this more general case does not have to take up oxygen).

OZONE: A form of oxygen whose molecules contain three atoms of oxygen. Ozone high in the atmosphere blocks harmful ultraviolet rays from the Sun, but at ground level it is an irritant gas when breathed in and so is regarded as a form of pollution. The ozone layer is the uppermost part of the stratosphere.

PAINT: A coating that has both decorative and protective properties, and that consists of a pigment suspended in a vehicle, or binder, made of a resin dissolved in a solvent. It dries to give a tough film.

PARTIAL PRESSURE: The pressure a gas in a mixture would exert if it alone occupied the flask. For example, oxygen makes up about a fifth of the atmosphere. Its partial pressure is therefore about a fifth of normal atmospheric pressure.

PASTE: A thick suspension of a solid in a liquid.

PATINA: A surface coating that develops on metals and protects them from further corrosion, for example, the green coating of copper carbonate that forms on copper statues.

PERIODIC TABLE: A chart organizing elements by atomic number and chemical properties into groups and periods.

PERMANENT HARDNESS: Hardness in the water that cannot be removed by boiling.

PETROCHEMICAL: Any of a large group of manufactured chemicals (not fuels) that come from petroleum and natural gas. It is usually taken to include similar products that can be made from coal and plants.

PETROLEUM: A natural mixture of a range of gases, liquids, and solids derived from the decomposed remains of animals and plants.

PHASE: A particular state of matter. A substance can exist as a solid, liquid, or gas and may change between these phases with the addition or removal of energy, usually in the form of heat.

PHOSPHOR: A material that glows when energized by ultraviolet or electron beams, such as in fluorescent tubes and cathode ray tubes.

PHOTOCHEMICAL SMOG: A mixture of tiny particles of dust and soot combined with a brown haze caused by the reaction of colorless nitric oxide from vehicle exhausts and oxygen of the air to form brown nitrogen dioxide.

PHOTOCHROMIC GLASSES: Glasses designed to change color with the intensity of light. They use the property that certain substances, for example, silver halide, can change color (and change chemically) in light. For example, when silver chromide is dispersed in the glass melt, sunlight decomposes the silver halide to release silver (and so darken the lens). But the halogen cannot escape; and when the light is removed, the halogen recombines with the silver to turn back to colorless silver halide.

PHOTOSYNTHESIS: The natural process that happens in green plants whereby the energy from light is used to help turn gases, water, and minerals into tissue and energy.

PIEZOELECTRICS: Materials that produce electric currents when they are deformed, or vice versa.

PIGMENT: Insoluble particles of coloring material.

PITH: The central strand of spongy tissue found in the stems of most plants.

PLASTIC: Material—a carbon-based substance consisting of long chains or networks (polymers) of simple molecules. The word plastic is commonly used only for synthetic polymers. Property—a material is plastic if it can be made to change shape easily and then remain in this new shape (contrast with elasticity and brittleness).

PLASTIC CHANGE: A permanent change in shape that happens without breaking.

PLASTICIZER: A chemical added to rubbers and resins to make it easier for them to be deformed and molded. Plasticizers are also added to cement to make it more easily worked when used as a mortar.

PLATE GLASS: Rolled, ground, and polished sheet glass.

PLIABLE: Supple enough to be repeatedly bent without fracturing.

PLYWOOD: An engineered wood laminate consisting of sheets of wood bonded with resin. Each sheet of wood has the grain at right angles to the one above and below. This imparts stability to the product.

PNEUMATIC DEVICE: Any device that works with air pressure.

POLAR: Something that has a partial electric charge.

POLYAMIDES: A compound that contains more than one amide group, for example, nylon.

POLYMER: A compound that is made of long chains or branching networks by combining molecules called monomers as repeating units. Poly means "many," mer means "part."

PORCELAIN: A hard, fine-grained, and translucent white ceramic that is made of china clay and is fired to a high temperature. Varieties include china.

PORES: Spaces between particles that are small enough to hold water by capillary action, but large enough to allow water to enter.

POROUS: A material that has small cavities in it, known as pores. These pores may or may not be joined. As a result, porous materials may or may not allow a liquid or gas to pass through them. Popularly, porous is used to mean permeable, the kind of porosity in which the pores are joined, and liquids or gases can flow.

POROUS CERAMICS: Ceramics that have not been fired at temperatures high enough to cause the clays to fuse and so prevent the slow movement of water.

POTENTIAL ENERGY: Energy due to the position of an object. Water in a reservoir has potential energy because it is stored up, and when released, it moves down to a lower level.

POWDER COATING: The application of a pigment in powder form without the use of a solvent.

POWDER FORMING: A process of using a powder to fill a mold and then heating the powder to make it fuse into a solid.

PRECIPITATE: A solid substance formed as a result of a chemical reaction between two liquids or gases.

PRESSURE: The force per unit area measured in SI units in Pascals and also more generally in atmospheres.

PRIMARY COLORS: A set of colors from which all others can be made. In transmitted light they are red, blue, and green.

PROTEIN: Substances in plants and animals that include nitrogen.

PROTON: A positively charged particle in the nucleus of an atom that balances out the charge of the surrounding electrons.

QUENCH: To put into water in order to cool rapidly.

RADIATION: The transmission of energy from one body to another without any contribution from the intervening space. *Contrast with* **CONVECTION** and **CONDUCTION**

RADIOACTIVE: A substance that spontaneously emits energetic particles.

RARE EARTHS: Any of a group of metal oxides that are found widely throughout the Earth's rocks, but in low concentrations. They are mainly made up of the elements of the lanthanide series of the periodic table of the elements.

RAW MATERIAL: A substance that has not been prepared, but that has an intended use in manufacturing.

RAY: Narrow beam of light.

RAYON: An artificial fiber made from natural cellulose.

REACTION (CHEMICAL): The recombination of two substances using parts of each substance.

REACTIVE: A substance that easily reacts with many other substances.

RECYCLE: To take once used materials and make them available for reuse.

REDUCTION, REDUCING AGENT: The removal of oxygen from or the addition of hydrogen to a compound.

REFINING: Separating a mixture into the simpler substances of which it is made, especially petrochemical refining.

REFRACTION: The bending of a ray of light as it passes between substances of different refractive index (light-bending properties).

REFRACTORY: Relating to the use of a ceramic material, especially a brick, in high-temperature conditions of, for example, a furnace.

REFRIGERANT: A substance that, on changing between a liquid and a gas, can absorb large amounts of (latent) heat from its surroundings.

REGENERATED FIBERS: Fibers that have been dissolved in a solution and then recovered from the solution in a different form.

REINFORCED FIBER: A fiber that is mixed with a resin, for example, glass-reinforced fiber.

RESIN: A semisolid natural material that is made of plant secretions and often yellow-brown in color. Also synthetic

materials with the same type of properties. Synthetic resins have taken over almost completely from natural resins and are available as thermoplastic resins and thermosetting resins.

RESPIRATION: The process of taking in oxygen and releasing carbon dioxide in animals and the reverse in plants.

RIVET: A small rod of metal that is inserted into two holes in metal sheets and then burred over at both ends in order to stick the sheets together.

ROCK: A naturally hard inorganic material composed of mineral particles or crystals.

ROLLING: The process in which metal is rolled into plates and bars.

ROSIN: A brittle form of resin used in varnishes.

RUST: The product of the corrosion of iron and steel in the presence of air and water.

SALT: Generally thought of as sodium chloride, common salt; however, more generally a salt is a compound involving a metal. There are therefore many "salts" in water in addition to sodium chloride.

SAPWOOD: The outer, living layers of the tree, which includes cells for the transportation of water and minerals between roots and leaves.

SATURATED: A state in which a liquid can hold no more of a substance dissolved in it.

SEALANTS: A material designed to stop water or other liquids from penetrating into a surface or between surfaces. Most sealants are adhesives.

SEMICONDUCTOR: A crystalline solid that has an electrical conductivity part way between a conductor and an insulator. This material can be altered by doping to control an electric current. Semiconductors are the basis of transistors, integrated circuits, and other modern electronic solid-state devices.

SEMIPERMEABLE MEMBRANE: A thin material that acts as a fine sieve or filter, allowing small molecules to pass, but holding back large molecules.

SEPARATING COLUMN: A tall glass tube containing a porous disk near the base and filled with a substance such as aluminum oxide that can absorb materials on its surface. When a mixture passes through the columns, fractions are retarded by differing amounts so that each fraction is washed through the column in sequence.

SEPARATING FUNNEL: A pear-shaped glass funnel designed to permit the separation of immiscible liquids by simply pouring off the more dense liquid from the bottom of the funnel, while leaving the less dense liquid in the funnel.

SHAKES: A defect in wood produced by the wood tissue separating, usually parallel to the rings.

SHEEN: A lustrous, shiny surface on a yarn. It is produced by the finishing process or may be a natural part of the yarn.

SHEET-METAL FORMING: The process of rolling out metal into sheet.

SILICA: Silicon dioxide, most commonly in the form of sand.

SILICA GLASS: Glass made exclusively of silica.

SINTER: The process of heating that makes grains of a ceramic or metal a solid mass before it becomes molten.

SIZE: A glue, varnish, resin, or similar very dilute adhesive sealant used to block up the pores in porous surfaces or, for example, plaster and paper. Once the size has dried, paint or other surface coatings can be applied without the coating sinking in.

SLAG: A mixture of substances that are waste products of a furnace. Most slag are mainly composed of silicates.

SMELTING: Roasting a substance in order to extract the metal contained in it.

SODA: A flux for glassmaking consisting of sodium carbonate.

SOFTWOOD: Wood obtained from a coniferous tree.

SOLID: A rigid form of matter that maintains its shape regardless of whether or not it is in a container.

SOLIDIFICATION: Changing from a liquid to a solid.

SOLUBILITY: The maximum amount of a substance that can be contained in a solvent.

SOLUBLE: Readily dissolvable in a solvent.

SOLUTION: A mixture of a liquid (the solvent) and at least one other substance of lesser abundance (the solute). Like all mixtures, solutions can be separated by physical means.

SOLVAY PROCESS: Modern method of manufacturing the industrial alkali sodium carbonate (soda ash).

SOLVENT: The main substance in a solution.

SPECTRUM: A progressive series arranged in order, for example, the range of colors that make up visible light as seen in a rainbow.

SPINNERET: A small metal nozzle perforated with many small holes through which a filament solution is forced. The filaments that emerge are solidified by cooling and the filaments twisted together to form a yarn.

SPINNING: The process of drawing out and twisting short fibers, for example, wool, and thus making a thread or yarn.

SPRING: A natural flow of water from the ground.

STABILIZER: A chemical that, when added to other chemicals, prevents further reactions. For example, in soda lime glass the lime acts as a stabilizer for the silica.

STAPLE: A short fiber that has to be twisted with other fibers (spun) in order to make a long thread or yarn.

STARCHES: One form of carbohydrate. Starches can be used to make adhesives.

STATE OF MATTER: The physical form of matter. There are three states of matter: liquid, solid, and gas.

STEAM: Water vapor at the boiling point of water.

STONEWARE: Nonwhite pottery that has been fired at a high temperature until some of the clay has fused, a state called vitrified. Vitrification makes the pottery impervious to water. It is used for general tableware, often for breakfast crockery.

STRAND: When a number of yarns are twisted together, they make a strand. Strands twisted together make a rope.

SUBSTANCE: A type of material including mixtures.

SULFIDE: A compound that is composed only of metal and sulfur atoms, for example, PbS, the mineral galena.

SUPERCONDUCTORS: Materials that will conduct electricity with virtually no resistance if they are cooled to temperatures close to absolute zero ($-273°C$).

SURFACE TENSION: The force that operates on the surface of a liquid, and that makes it act as though it were covered with an invisible elastic film.

SURFACTANT: A substance that acts on a surface, such as a detergent.

SUSPENDED, SUSPENSION: Tiny particles in a liquid or a gas that do not settle out with time.

SYNTHETIC: Something that does not occur naturally but has to be manufactured. Synthetics are often produced from materials that do not occur in nature, for example, from petrochemicals. (i) Dye—a synthetic dye is made from petrochemicals, as opposed to natural dyes that are made of extracts of plants. (ii) Fiber—synthetic is a subdivision of artificial. Although both polyester and rayon are artificial fibers, rayon is made from reconstituted natural cellulose fibers and so is not synthetic, while polyester is made from petrochemicals and so is a synthetic fiber.

TANNIN: A group of pale-yellow or light-brown substances derived from plants that are used in dyeing fabric and making ink. Tannins are soluble in water and produce dark-blue or dark-green solutions when added to iron compounds.

TARNISH: A coating that develops as a result of the reaction between a metal and the substances in the air. The most common form of tarnishing is a very thin transparent oxide coating, such as occurs on aluminum. Sulfur compounds in the air make silver tarnish black.

TEMPER: To moderate or to make stronger: used in the metal industry to describe softening hardened steel or cast iron by reheating at a lower temperature or to describe hardening steel by reheating and cooling in oil; in the glass industry, to describe toughening glass by first heating it and then slowly cooling it.

TEMPORARILY HARD WATER: Hard water that contains dissolved substances that can be removed by boiling.

TENSILE (PULLING STRENGTH): The greatest lengthwise (pulling) stress a substance can bear without tearing apart.

TENSION: A state of being pulled. Compare to compression.

TERRA COTTA: Red earth-colored glazed or unglazed fired clay whose origins lie in the Mediterranean region of Europe.

THERMOPLASTIC: A plastic that will soften and can be molded repeatedly into different shapes. It will then set into the molded shape as it cools.

THERMOSET: A plastic that will set into a molded shape as it first cools, but that cannot be made soft again by reheating.

THREAD: A long length of filament, group of filaments twisted together, or a long length of short fibers that have been spun and twisted together into a continuous strand.

TIMBER: A general term for wood suitable for building or for carpentry and consisting of roughcut planks.
Compare to **LUMBER**

TRANSITION METALS: Any of the group of metallic elements (for example, chromium and iron) that belong to the central part of the periodic table of the elements and whose oxides commonly occur in a variety of colors.

TRANSPARENT: Something that will readily let light through, for example, window glass. Compare to translucent, when only some light gets through but an image cannot be seen, for example, greaseproof paper.

TROPOSPHERE: The lower part of the atmosphere in which clouds form. In general, temperature decreases with height.

TRUNK: The main stem of a tree.

VACUUM: Something from which all air has been removed.

VAPOR: The gaseous phase of a substance that is a liquid or a solid at that temperature, for example, water vapor is the gaseous form of water.

VAPORIZE: To change from a liquid to a gas, or vapor.

VENEER: A thin sheet of highly decorative wood that is applied to cheap wood or engineered wood products to improve their appearance and value.

VINYL: Often used as a general name for plastic. Strictly, vinyls are polymers derived from ethylene by removal of one hydrogen atom, for example, PVC, polyvinylchloride.

VISCOSE: A yellow-brown solution made by treating cellulose with alkali solution and carbon disulfide and used to make rayon.

VISCOUS, VISCOSITY: Sticky. Viscosity is a measure of the resistance of a liquid to flow. The higher the viscosity—the more viscous it is—the less easily it will flow.

VITREOUS CHINA: A translucent form of china or porcelain.

VITRIFICATION: To heat until a substance changes into a glassy form and fuses together.

VOLATILE: Readily forms a gas. Some parts of a liquid mixture are often volatile, as is the case for crude oil. This allows them to be separated by distillation.

WATER CYCLE: The continual interchange of water between the oceans, the air, clouds, rain, rivers, ice sheets, soil, and rocks.

WATER VAPOR: The gaseous form of water.

WAVELENGTH: The distance between adjacent crests on a wave. Shorter wavelengths have smaller distances between crests than longer wavelengths.

WAX: Substances of animal, plant, mineral, or synthetic origin that are similar to fats but are less greasy and harder. They form hard films that can be polished.

WEAVING: A way of making a fabric by passing two sets of yarns through one another at right angles to make a kind of tight meshed net with no spaces between the yarns.

WELDING: Technique used for joining metal pieces through intense localized heat. Welding often involves the use of a joining metal such as a rod of steel used to attach steel pieces (arc welding).

WETTING: In adhesive spreading, a term that refers to the complete coverage of an adhesive over a surface.

WETTING AGENT: A substance that is able to cover a surface completely with a film of liquid. It is a substance with a very low surface tension.

WHITE GLASS: Also known as milk glass, it is an opaque white glass that was originally made in Venice and meant to look like porcelain.

WROUGHT IRON: A form of iron that is relatively soft and can be bent without breaking. It contains less than 0.1% carbon.

YARN: A strand of fibers twisted together and used to make textiles.

Set Index